Greenham Women Everywhere

Dreams, Ideas and Actions from the Women's Peace Movement

Alice Cook & Gwyn Kirk

South End Press

First published in 1983 by Pluto Press Limited,
The Works, 105A Torriano Avenue, London NW5 2RX
and simultaneously in the USA by South End Press,
302 Columbus Avenue, Boston, Massachusetts 02116

Second impression 1984

Typeset by Wayside Graphics, Clevedon, Avon
Printed in Great Britain by Photobooks (Bristol) Limited
Bound by W.H. Ware & Sons, Tweed Road,
Clevedon, Avon

Cover illustration by Saša Marinkov
Designed by Kate Hepburn

ISBN 0-89608-199-0

Contents

RAF Greenham Common is used by the US Air Force as part of a NATO agreement. At present, there is no obligation for the US government to obtain Britain's consent before firing missiles from Greenham Common. Hence the base is referred to in the text as 'USAF Greenham Common'.

Introduction

Greenham Common women's peace camp has existed now (June 1983) for 21 months, maintaining an unbroken presence outside the air base, despite two bad winters and continual harassment by the authorities. The ideas and vitality exemplified by the peace camp are in dramatic contrast to the bleakness and dreadful purpose of the base – two opposing value systems right next to one another but on opposite sides of the fence. The peace camp is a remarkable manifestation of women's determination and vision, an inspiration to many thousands of people in this country and abroad. As well as being a round-the-clock protest against cruise missiles, it is also a resource – a women's space in which to try to live out ideals of feminism and nonviolence, a focus for information and ideas, a meeting place, and a vital context for women to express their beliefs and feelings.

The peace camp does not exist in isolation, but is supported by a wide network of individuals, women's groups, peace groups, CND groups, religious groups and union branches, who send money, food, warm clothes, firewood, equipment, and offer their homes, telephones, cars, time and energy. Thousands of people all over the world have sent letters, cards and telegrams of support and encouragement. It is a testimony to people's support for the peace camp that it has existed almost entirely on donations since the beginning.

Through contact with the peace camp and the actions associated with it, many women have discovered that they are not alone in their beliefs or their fears for the future. This growing network of women is a source of inspiration and strength to us. Like so many women, we have found this a context where we can express our opposition to the diabolical madness of the arms race.

Women outside the main gate, USAF Greenham Common

Eleni Leoussi

Opposing cruise missiles

The growth of the peace movement in Britain and Western Europe was stimulated by NATO's decision of December 1979 to site US cruise and Pershing II missiles in several European countries in the 1980s. This decision gave rise to sickening discussions on the possibility of a 'limited nuclear war' in Europe. In addition, the British government's commitment to Trident submarine-launched nuclear missiles to replace and 'upgrade' the existing Polaris system – and to be paid for by British taxpayers – is another major focus for opposition in this country.

Like most government decisions, the decision about cruise missiles was taken over our heads and without our knowledge. It was also taken over the heads of most MPs, our elected representatives, despite the fact that the government purports to be acting in our name, defending 'freedom and democracy'. It is the presence of 20 or so peace camps outside military bases, and the campaign of nonviolent direct action associated with them, which has been largely responsible for opening up a public debate about cruise missiles and disarmament in general. As the first peace camp in this country, Greenham Common women's peace camp has played a special part in this. Also, following the lead taken by the peace camps, the Campaign for Nuclear Disarmament (CND) has supported and organised nonviolent direct action at national level for the first time in its 25-year history – a recognition of the ineffectiveness of going through the 'proper channels'.

The issue of cruise and Trident missiles and nuclear disarmament did eventually surface 'officially' in the 1983 general election, thus breaking the political consensus on defence which had lasted for 20 years. Disarmament was a central issue for the Labour Party, reflecting growing public awareness and deep concern over the escalation of the arms race. However, this issue was apparently not sufficiently important to people to win the election for Labour. Indeed, the new Conservative government, firmly committed to cruise missiles and increased defence spending, will interpret its election success as a clear mandate for its defence policies and will feel even more confident than before about suppressing opposition to nuclear weapons. Despite the Conservative election victory, the majority of people in this country are against cruise missiles (54 per cent, according to a Gallup poll published in the *Daily Telegraph* in February 1983), including a group called Tories against Cruise and Trident.

Mrs Thatcher's commitment to US military policy is as uncritical as it is uncompromising and her re-election is undoubtedly a major setback for the peace movement. Even if a Labour government had been elected, crucial differences of opinion would still have existed between Labour politicians as to what they would do about disarmament. A Labour government would have been under great pressure not to depart from existing military commitments both from within its own ranks, and from British military and financial institutions, and international organisations such as the EEC and the International Monetary Fund, both dominated by the United States.

In discussing the campaign against cruise missiles it is as well to acknowledge some of the realities of the situation at the outset. Cruise missiles are pilotless aircraft, each carrying one nuclear warhead, launched either from sea, ground or air. Their maximum range is 1,500 miles and, once fired, they travel at about 500 miles per hour. They fly very low, thus eluding enemy radar, and find their target by means of a computerised map which matches the terrain to radar altitude readings.

There are 4,000 cruise missiles being produced and the plan is to deploy 464 land-based cruise missiles in Europe: 96 at Greenham Common; 64 at Molesworth; 112 at Comiso in Sicily; 96 in West Germany; 48 in Holland; and 48 in Belgium.

If they are as accurate as their makers claim, cruise missiles could hit military as well as civilian targets in the USSR. They could also be used to fight a nuclear war in Europe, and would make the escalation from the use of conventional to nuclear weapons easier. The missiles stationed at Comiso will have the capacity to hit Middle Eastern targets, thus heightening the possibility that US nuclear weapons could be used to intervene in a Middle Eastern conflict.

Each one of these 464 cruise missiles would have the capacity to destroy 15 towns the size of Hiroshima. The official scenario is that, in times of grave international tension, the missiles and their warheads would be taken from their silos and loaded on to trucks. A cavalcade of US troops, tanks, the 55-foot long launching vehicle and a security system protecting even against chemical weapons, would accompany the bombs through the countryside. They would thus avoid the possibility of being destroyed in their silos, and in their new positions would be free to destroy areas of the Soviet Union, Eastern Europe, or other pre-programmed targets. At Greenham, there will be a unit of 12 men (called Quick Reaction Alert) constantly on alert in one of the silos, ready to put this scenario into action at any time should the order be given.

The fact that cruise missiles will not be launched from Greenham but from somewhere within a 50 to 100 mile radius, makes that entire area a likely target. This highlights the irony of talk of cruise missiles as 'defensive' weapons. Far from being protected by them, the very fact that there will be 96 at Greenham (and 464 in Europe as a whole) means that this entire area is more vulnerable to attack. While Soviet surveillance systems are not yet able to detect cruise missiles once in flight (although within the next two years it is expected that they will be able to) they would receive satellite information when the missiles were taken from their silos and transported around the countryside.

The missile silos at Greenham Common – enormous mounds of reinforced concrete – are nearly complete. Cruise missiles and their launching lorries can be brought into the base by air. Blockades of the base, though of great symbolic importance in showing the strength of people's opposition, cannot physically stop cruise missiles. Blockades would have to be *massive*, recurrent and planned entirely without police knowledge to disrupt the functioning of the base substantially. Virtually every day for at least the last 18 months, huge container lorries have been going in and out of the air base. Some people believe that much of the equipment needed for the missiles, and perhaps the missiles themselves – though without their nuclear warheads – may be at Greenham Common already.

The two superpowers, the USA and USSR, have been developing more and more sophisticated weapons and guidance and detection systems for decades. There is much discussion and argument as to the strength of these arsenals, each side underestimating its own capacity and overestimating the capacity of the other, seemingly to justify continued escalation of the arms race. The economies of both superpowers are in effect war economies, where vast wealth is invested in the research and development of ever more deadly weapons systems, and literally millions of people are involved in this process in some way. In the West, private companies make enormous profits at every step: mining uranium, processing it and enriching it to 'weapon grade' plutonium, designing and producing the various components, and so on. In the Soviet bloc this process is organised through state departments and industrial enterprises.

It is against this background that the superpowers talk about disarmament. Not surprisingly, political and economic systems so heavily dependent on arms industries produce more weapons, not fewer. Years of sporadic talks have got virtually nowhere. Both major power blocs continue utterly entrenched in their existing commitments. It has been said that if there is some agreement in the current round of arms limitation talks in Geneva this year, NATO will not deploy cruise missiles in Europe, but such agreement is hardly likely. What is needed is intervention at every stage in the process: millions of people making clear their opposition by, for example, putting political pressure on governments, refusing to make the various components for the missiles, refusing to transport or assemble them, and refusing to build the silos or supply materials.

At the beginning of June 1983, NATO defence ministers confirmed their earlier decision to deploy cruise and Pershing II missiles if the Geneva negotiations fail, but Denmark and Greece both had reservations and Spain abstained. The Dutch government is openly debating whether to reduce its nuclear role in NATO and has not yet agreed that cruise missiles should be deployed in Holland. US Assistant Secretary for Defense Richard Perle said that the decision to site cruise and Pershing II missiles in Europe had 'proved politically difficult to implement.' (The *Guardian*, 3 June 1983.)

The governments of Western democracies depend on people's consent for their legitimacy. The great majority of people support the government, if not wholeheartedly then tacitly, by not objecting to what it does. Over the past two or three years many people have begun to question a 'defence' policy which needs ever more horrendous weapons at enormous expense. There are now enough nuclear weapons in the world to totally destroy a city the size of Cardiff every half hour for the next 57 years. Indeed, there are sufficient to destroy the whole world many times over. More and more people – women particularly – are recognising that the only hope we have of reversing this terrifying situation is to withdraw our support from a system which in no way deserves our co-operation or respect.

Greenham Common women's peace camp is an initiative by a small group of women who felt desperate about the prospect of cruise missiles being sited in this country, convinced that this would make Britain more of a target than ever, and angry that resources are being squandered on weapons of mass destruction. It is the strength of these ideas which inspired us to write this book. It speaks in a variety of voices as different women describe their dreams, explain their ideas and experiences, and express their fears, optimism and vision. More and more women are acknowledging their fear of nuclear weapons and gaining confidence to take action. This is a struggle not only for survival but for a life worth living – a life not continually overshadowed by the very real possibility of annihilation through nuclear war.

Fear is the starting point and, given the dreadful potential of nuclear weapons, it is absolutely reasonable to be afraid.

A private nightmare

As a person who has lived most of their life, I still do not wish to die by lingering on with some form of radiation sickness. I worry when I look at my dear grandchildren and my heart aches – will they ever have the chance to grow up? I worry about this beautiful earth of ours, it belongs to all of us, why should it be destroyed by the few?

This fear is on my mind every day, and I have dreams about the terrible slaughter and burning up a nuclear war would bring. My most recent dream was:

I was walking along a long road, weeping and looking for my husband. The earth was opening up, and the bodies of thousands of screaming naked people were falling into this abyss.

All members of my family and friends worry about this third world war happening, especially the young people with children. I think some of them are living in dread. I know lots of people try to push this into the back of their minds, but I think it is getting harder to keep it there now. I'm sure most people are getting the feeling that we are heading towards some dreadful calamity.

Mrs Smith

The horror of nuclear weapons and the possibility of nuclear war had frightened and worried me [Alice] for years. I chose the people I discussed this with. Many men laughed off my bad dreams, until I stopped bothering to talk about it to them. I had a feeling that many women felt as I did, however, and finally put an advertisement in *Spare Rib*, asking women to contact me if they had had dreams about nuclear war. All through that summer in 1980, I received letter after letter from women talking about their own bad dreams. Later, I put a similar advertisement in *Sanity*, which is read by men as well as women. The response was so immediate and so many women replied that I began to get a strong sense of an undercurrent of anxiety, which was having far-reaching effects on people's lives. This anxiety emerged in dreams and worried thoughts, plans for the future and an overriding feeling of desperation and pessimism.

I don't think about the future any more. I never think more than a year ahead. I can't conceive of the future and I think it's a result of the fear of war. I've been aware of the bomb since I was eight or nine. I was very frightened then but I suppose I got used to it. But now I can't conceive of the 1990s; I feel I mustn't sink into thinking like that but I can't help it. Then I think that I'm not going to sacrifice anything now, any sort of enjoyment I might have, for the sake of the future. That's why I work hard for a while and then stop, because there seems no point. I run the risk of people saying I'm crazy, but I can't stay with anything because I want to do as many things as I can. I find I don't want to get closely involved with anyone. It's hard to think of people you know dying. I've got my family to think about and I don't want any more worries. I don't want to think about anyone else dying.

I think that the fear of war has increased in the last couple of years, and I'm sure I'm not the only one to have private nightmares about it. My dreams about war are all quite similar. They take place after the bomb has dropped, and involve people running around madly, trying to get away. Or else everyone is dead and I'm alone, trying to look for someone I know. In the dreams, I know there's no escape and that to run around blindly is pointless. All I want is to find someone and die with someone I know. I always feel an incredible desolation, a sense of loss, that all these people are going to be dead in a short while, myself included.
Ruth

No one knows just how many people have repeated nightmares about the nuclear holocaust. Such dreams highlight the enormous strength of feeling which, if it could be acknowledged and mobilised, would be freed for positive action. One of the most common features of the letters was that each woman felt completely alone in her fear. She had no idea that other women felt the same. This was before the women's peace movement became such a growing force. At the time, there seemed no positive way in which this energy could be channelled. Most of the women's dreams and statements that appear in this chapter date from that time. Since then, I and many of the women who replied have been able to turn this energy outwards in a positive direction and become actively involved in the women's peace movement.

Many women who have visited the women's peace camp at Greenham Common, or become involved in actions associated with it, have done so after a period of growing fear and anxiety about nuclear war. These fears are not much talked about. They usually remain the private concern of individuals too nervous of being thought hysterical to share them with others. We have to try to come terms with these dreadful feelings of despair and paralysis or else we are submerged by them. What propels people into action is that the feeling of impotence becomes so unbearable that we have to try to do something about it.

The press characterises women's actions at Greenham and elsewhere as 'naive', 'sincere', 'emotional', thus seeking to denigrate them by using attributes that are thought to be 'female' or weak. What is left out of their stories is that this kind of response is not the easy option it is believed to be. It is easier to think about cruise missiles in the abstract language of political debate, where death is discussed in facts and figures, than to think about one person's death from radiation sickness. In order to be able to respond emotionally to the fact that our planet may be destroyed by nuclear weapons, each person must struggle through the layers of apathy and paralysis that surround this issue.

Many people believe that a nuclear war is more likely now than at any other time since the Cuba crisis of 1962. People see the cold war re-spiralling. Through newspapers and television they get a picture of Reagan and Andropov becoming increasingly intransigent, increasingly hostile to arms reduction, warning of war. According to recent opinion polls (The *Observer*, NOP, 8 November 1981, and The *Guardian*, Marplan, 24 January 1983):

49% of people interviewed think a nuclear war is likely in their lifetime

87% believe they and their families would not survive if nuclear weapons were used against Britain

57% think US defence policy is making nuclear war more likely

53% think American bases should be removed from Britain

58% of women do not want Trident nuclear submarines

67% of women do not want cruise missiles

We are repeatedly told of the importance of a nuclear deterrent against the Soviet threat, but many people now fear the USA almost as much as the USSR. More people in Britain are now in favour of unilateral disarmament than ever before.

In an opinion poll conducted by *New Society* in 1980 most people who said they were worried about nuclear weapons were either unwilling to do anything, or felt that nothing could be done. Many people are both anxious and fatalistic about the nuclear war they increasingly expect, and are increasingly certain that they will not survive. If the findings of the various polls are turned into personal statements they have a very different impact.

I worry about nuclear weapons.

I believe a nuclear war will happen in my lifetime.

If there is a nuclear war, I am sure I will die. I will either die from the initial blast, be vaporised or crushed, or I will die in the ensuing weeks from radiation sickness.

To confront the issue like this turns the abstract into the concrete, the impersonal into the personal. This is the reality behind the beliefs stated in the opinion polls, because the use of nuclear weapons will **directly** and **personally** affect every individual.

We all live with the threat of nuclear war. It is a fact of life, a possibility that permeates our lives whether we choose to think about it or not. At this minute there are enough nuclear weapons targeted on various countries to blow up the world many times over, were a war to be started by accident or design. We are surrounded by information that tries to block out this fact. Nuclear terminology – words like 'overkill', 'megaton', 'theatre war' – has become commonplace. Even the image of a nuclear explosion, the mushroom cloud, is a term in general use. We read not of nuclear weapons and what they actually do, but of abstract 'warheads'. In the debate over cruise missiles, for example, the government has focused on 'dual key control' and how 'cruise is an answer to the Soviet SS20s'. This euphemistic argument leads to a curious sense of unreality, when we realise that what is being talked about is the deaths of millions of people.

It is, of course, in the interests of those politicians who support the nuclear arms race to ignore stark realities in their presentation of the 'facts' to the people, and to concentrate on euphemisms instead. It is also not surprising that most of us accept this with a certain amount of relief. What we have to come to terms with otherwise is a picture so terrifying that our whole being revolts against it and we develop mental strategies to defend ourselves.

But many people are finding it increasingly difficult to ward off their fear. Often it comes out in nightmares. In dreams we may deal with information and feelings which we cannot assimilate in waking life. The women who describe their dreams in the following pages often felt them to be a way of expressing to themselves fears that were too desolating to consider while awake.

It was a bright, grey winter's day. There was, to my certain knowledge, half an hour to go before the bomb dropped. I was walking, stumbling down a country lane, naked hawthorns on either side. I was with my two children. I felt at once calm, philosophic. There's only half an hour to go anyway. I mustn't frighten the children. I felt how easy it would be to die. Somehow personal annihilation was no threat. I could cope with death, whether it came suddenly and unknowingly, or slowly and tragically, watching my dearest girls ill, knowing my far-flung unreachable friends and family to be suffering too. If only. 'If only' was the crunch. 'If only' meant if only I could know that the sick fields and waters, trees and mountains could renew some day, if only the bare hawthorns could leaf again. So thinking I looked lovingly at the twigs and branches. Clearly, in sharp tender focus, young small green leaves sprang into sight. Their pale unfurling vulnerability, their promise of hope, their pledge of spring and rebirth, pierced me with emotion. I still knew there was half an hour to go, and that the world could not, would not revive. The eternal promise of the leaves had been betrayed,
and I awoke. I was startled to find that my predominant emotion was that of wonder and gratitude that I had been able to see those beautiful leaves before the world died.
Kate

I was in a jeep driving through a very wasted landscape. It looked like a desert but I knew it was a long time after a nuclear war. I was going away from one area to somewhere safer, but everywhere looked very blasted, like the Great Salt Lake of Utah, but it was just what had happened to the landscape as a result of the war.

The atmosphere was very thick. I couldn't see any stars, but the headlights of the jeep were working. I was driving along with someone else, who seemed to be a friend, but I couldn't tell the sex of the person. There was some trouble with the jeep, and it seemed fairly unlikely that we would get to our destination, which I felt to be London or some other big city, because there wouldn't be enough petrol.

My friend was driving, and I was holding between my knees a giant piece of ice. Inside the block there was a fish, and this was the last fish, which I had to get to London, which was the last place where there was still some clean water where the fish could survive. [A mythological character, Finn McClure, is told about a certain fish by an old woman. This is the fish of knowledge, the idea being that real power is knowledge and real knowledge is in the thoughts and words of creatures, stones and trees. Finn McClure catches the fish and by eating it gains the knowledge.]

This fish I was holding was the fish of knowledge, and if we could keep the fish alive there was some hope for continuance in the world. But if we couldn't it would be the end. There was a feeling that this was necessary, it was inevitable, we had to do it, it was all we could do, but the likelihood of actually doing it was fairly remote. The heat from the engine was starting to melt the ice, and I had to keep shifting it, and try to steer by non-existent stars.

When I woke up – still on the journey – I felt quite calm.
Noa

I have dreamt many times of the first few moments after a nuclear explosion.
On one occasion there was a horrible smell of burning flesh (although I have no idea what burning flesh smells like). Children were screaming, running with their hands lifted up for help, and their skin was peeling off. There was no blood. In fact there was no liquid, everything was hot and dry. I was somehow watching all this.
The dreams started after showing *The War Game* to children at the school where I teach. I'd seen the film eight years ago, but this time it was more shocking, more immediate. The kids were appalled and frightened, but on the surface I switched off. The

17

only way to cope was to cut off from it because it is so horrific. Two weeks later I dreamt about nuclear war four nights in succession. I still have the dreams sometimes but wake up with a different feeling. At the time it was fear. I'd wake up and realise that the war must already be here. It's in our heads and we are thinking and dreaming and making plans. Now I don't feel that kind of panic, I think I've accepted it, and that it's in everyone's heads. My mother, who lives in a totally different environment, talks about it, asking me if I think nuclear war will be so different from the last war.

They – men, the powers that be – have won the war already in a way, by planting it in our heads . . . The problem is so monumental that it tends to make action seem meaningless. Strength of numbers is nothing. Feeling so impotent and powerless adds to the guilt which I feel surrounds the whole issue.

There are times when walking down the street, touching things, the concrete, I think this is all going to go. It's disbelief, and once I get through the disbelief, panic. When I go it's never going to be replaced, it's the end.

There isn't the language to deal with this. It's like trying to imagine infinity. It's so vast that I am totally pessimistic. I go on marches in a very half-hearted way, knowing that at the end I'm just going to feel very depressed and panicky.

It's incredible that I or anybody else is talking about accepting it, almost tolerating it, but having exhausted the possibilities I can see no way out.

I'm very conscious of not reading or finding out more. It's bad enough dreaming about it. Men I know haven't ever described that feeling of panic, which women talk about – all the women I know have felt real fear over this threat. Of course they have a different perspective.

In the cold light of day I feel numb. It's not going to get me because I've accepted it, but in the dreams it's still full of panic and disbelief. Although I see myself in the dream, I don't feel myself in it and I'm incredulous. The strangest thing about the dreams, and the connection between them and how I feel about them when I'm awake is acceptance. We all take the image that is given to us. While I resent that I'm drawn into it, feel so angry about it, I live in this society and must take some of the blame for the feeling of inevitability that surrounds this issue.

Many years ago now, I had a nervous breakdown which

started with an anxiety attack in which I felt I couldn't breathe. I remember vividly the feeling – the same as in the dreams and when I think about war – total horror and panic, and yet tolerance at the same time. In the dream the siren goes off and I can watch the panic rising. I know that I can either surrender to the panic, or sit down and somehow refuse to be sucked into that state. When I wake up I won't allow that panic to get to me. But when I had the breakdown I felt somewhere deep inside that I had made a choice, wanted to be a victim of fear and panic, that it was somehow easier than the other choice.

Carol

Individuals have to come to terms – however they can – with living in a world under threat of total annihilation. Many simply drive it out of their consciousness, and those who try to confront this reality can run the risk that others will call them mad.

Women run that risk in any case:

16 times as many women as men are treated for depression;
many more women than men have 'breakdowns';
one out of every eight women spends time in mental hospitals;
millions are prescribed tranquillisers every year.

We are facing the ultimate insanity – destroying the world we live in. This insanity is the 'real' world. Yet if women talk plainly about how this insanity affects their lives now, before the event, they are called mad themselves.

So many people are depressed. They can't see a way of getting out of the terrible situation we're all in, where all our lives are threatened, and some people have severe mental problems from this. I was working in a psychiatric hostel for a couple of years before I gave up my job to come here [Greenham], and people were actually having breakdowns because of the violence of society. One woman I was working with was having nightmares every night about the nuclear disaster, the end of the world, and it meant that she just couldn't carry on with her ordinary life because it was meaningless to her, because she felt so hopeless, that there was nothing she could do about it. She'd collapsed under that pressure and had been labelled mad and locked away because of it. Supposedly for her protection, she'd been pumped full of drugs and put away from society.

She *knew* the reality. She just let it in and that was why it was so devastating for her, because she was isolated in that position. The attitude of the authorities was very much: don't talk to her about that because it'll just drive her more insane, whereas we should all have been admitting that this affects us all. She wasn't *mad* to be having breakdowns about it. We should all be changing society so no one needs to have a breakdown.
Sarah

Nobody really knows the effects of these bombs. It seems like the biggest gamble that we could possibly ever take, and here we are, it's happening now. The politicians want to hide away from the reality of the situation we're in. They're in it as deep as everybody else. They're just part of the whole spiral that's taking us down. It's as if there's a certain part of their personality that can't look at the reality of what's happening and can't look realistically at the part they're playing in that reality.

We fear many, many things, nuclear weapons being one, and it's necessary to block off things that really are so dreadful . . . we split off certain sections of our lives. We're taught right from beginning school. We begin to section off our thinking into certain avenues until, at the end of school life, children are specialising, they're going into different rooms to think about different things. They have different teachers to talk about different subjects. When you compartment your feelings it's a certain way of thinking that brings about a neurosis. That's all right on a temporary basis, but it doesn't help the *whole* person, the *whole* mind, the *whole* life, and neurosis will out, eventually. I think it's very important for people to start trying to face the situation and at least allow themselves to feel the truth and the reality of it.
Jayne

Dreams have brought the whole subject home to me in a way that thinking about the possibility has never done, because they make me feel so helpless. I am frightened in the dreams about my own survival and the survival of the people who are close to me, but what sets them apart from other anxiety dreams is the way they involve everyone and everything.
In one dream I am with my friend, and we are standing with crowds of

people outside, and we are all watching the sky. It is as if we know something is going to happen; there is a portentous feeling, we all know the bomb is going to drop, but can do nothing about it. It makes me feel empty and desolate, like stone — and this is the feeling I wake up with which makes the dream so hideous. It's a very different feeling from being emotional and upset: that tears up my stomach. This is far away from that kind of gut feeling, there is not even that response left, and that is what makes me feel so desperate. Knowing that everyone else is going to die makes the horror of the dreams seem all-embracing, somehow bigger. I watch other people in horror, although I feel it most in myself. I think of my insides, I don't think of anyone else's insides.

I wake up from such dreams in a state of shock and they stay with me for a long time afterwards. I wake up thinking, this is the end of the world. I don't think this is the end of me, or the end of England, but the end of the world, even though I can't possibly absorb this thought. I don't even know what it means. I wake up and the reality of the dream is far worse than the dream itself. I know that I have dreamt the palest reflection of what would happen.

They make me feel as if I should be listening to them in some way and I just don't know in what way. There is the possibility that they are a vehicle to release the worry I feel but am not always aware of. I'm cynical about the thought that I am dreaming about something that is going to happen.

But waking up after such dreams isn't a relief because of their content. I'm just as horrified when I wake up and know that these images are in my head.

Wendy

One of the ways we normally differentiate ourselves from our dreams is by a process of reality testing: we test the reality of the world we have woken up into against the reality of the dream world we have left. We wake up and realise that the monsters who pursued us such a short time ago are not actually in the room. We perceive that our life is not actually threatened in the way it seemed in the dream. The more frightening the dream and the more overwhelming the anxiety, the harder this process is, as anyone who has ever woken in terror from a nightmare will acknowledge. Dreams about nuclear war are different in this respect from other dreams. There is no waking up from this nightmare. We wake and know that the threat of nuclear war is a real one.

Yet politicians suggest that people need not worry, that they should have faith in a government which has rationally considered the options and decided that disarmament is naive and deluded. In a debate in parliament, John Nott, then minister of defence, claimed that he:

> knew of the apprehensions about nuclear war among ordinary people, worried about their children's future. But these natural apprehensions were misplaced provided Britain stuck to her course and did not gamble wildly on some different one.
>
> *The Times*, 4 March 1981

We are told not to worry, that our deaths are not our concern, and that we should leave the matter to politicians and nuclear strategists who are all the time planning and preparing for war. The government requires local councils to make plans for their areas: to work out how they would keep essential services running, organise civil defence training, provide emergency centres and decide which open spaces to use as mass burial and cremation sites. Many councils are convinced that such proposals are no more than a cruel confidence trick and that there is no defence against nuclear weapons. This is brought out in the following extracts from the *Emergency War Plan*, published by Lambeth Council, London.

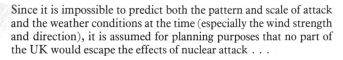

Since it is impossible to predict both the pattern and scale of attack and the weather conditions at the time (especially the wind strength and direction), it is assumed for planning purposes that no part of the UK would escape the effects of nuclear attack . . .

Post-Attack . . .
There may be extensive disruption to the normal services of water supply, waste disposal, refuse collection, sewerage, and fuel and energy supplies.

There may be large numbers of casualties lying where they had died, and large numbers of survivors may be living in conditions in which peacetime standards of hygiene would be difficult or impossible to achieve.

Until more usual and permanent arrangements could be made for the resumption of . . . services . . . , the rapid improvisation of public emergency sanitary measures would be of paramount importance. These measures may include:

- The collection of the dead.
- The disposal of the dead, probably by mass interment or cremation without formal identification.
- The collection and disposal of human waste.
- The collection and disposal of refuse.

- The provision of communal sanitary facilities.
- The provision of communal cooking (in co-operation with the Borough Emergency Feeding Officer) and water storage facilities . . .

Radiation Malaise
Persons exposed to 'radiation' from fallout may contract radiation malaise, the severity being dependent upon the intensity of the dose. The signs and symptoms of the malaise are initially nausea, vomiting, diarrhoea, headaches, apathy and dehydration; in severe cases after a latent period of about a week the following signs will appear:
- diarrhoea with blood in stools,
- fever,
- haemorrhage from all skin surfaces,
- ulceration of tongue, throat and bowels,
- loss of hair . . .

Emergency Feeding . . . 6: Emergency feeding will not be commenced until the radiation hazard has reached acceptable levels; until that time householders and others must exist on stocks of food and water stored in the refuge room prior to attack. On being instructed to commence emergency feeding operations it will be necessary to ensure that food, water and outside areas to be used are decontaminated. The following guidance is given: . . . Special protective clothing will not be issued. Exposed parts of the body should be carefully washed with soap and water . . .

Compare the view that radioactive fallout is something we can just wash off, with Dr Helen Caldicott talking about the effects of plutonium which would be released into the atmosphere after a nuclear explosion and which is very easily absorbed into our bodies – our blood, bones and internal organs.

Plutonium is one of the most carcinogenic substances known . . . One pound, if uniformly distributed, could hypothetically induce lung cancer in every person on earth . . . [it] has a half-life of 24,400 years and, once created, remains poisonous for at least half a million years.

Plutonium is a chemically reactive metal which, if exposed to air, ignites spontaneously to produce respirable particles of plutonium dioxide . . . These particles can be transported by atmospheric currents and inhaled by people and animals. When lodged in the tiny airways of the lung, plutonium particles bombard surrounding tissues with alpha radiation. Smaller particles may break away to be absorbed through the lung and enter the bloodstream. Because plutonium has properties similar to those of iron, it is combined with the iron-transporting proteins in the blood and conveyed to iron storage cells in the liver and bone marrow. Here, too, it irradiates

23

nearby cells, inducing liver and bone cancer, and leukaemia.

Plutonium's ironlike properties also permit the element to cross the highly selective placental barrier and reach the developing foetus, possibly causing . . . gross deformities in the newborn infant. Plutonium is concentrated by the testicles and ovaries, where inevitably it will cause genetic mutations which will be passed on to future generations.

Dr Helen Caldicott, *Nuclear Madness*

Thus children born to people whose parents survived Hiroshima are more likely to be born deformed; the radioactive particles which are absorbed so easily into the body are still active years later.

Our skin absorbs these radioactive particles.

They sink into the earth.

They are absorbed by all animal and plant life.

The danger lives on for thousands of years, lessening only gradually.

The people of Hiroshima are separated from us by 40 years and half the world. They are still dying from the effects of that 'small' bomb.

Each cruise missile is 15 times as lethal as the bomb that was dropped on Hiroshima.

The prospect of a nuclear war is so terrifying that we refuse to think about it. It is easier to be numb than to consider what we can do to prevent the use of these weapons and stop the mentality that fuels the arms race. It is as if we are frozen.

I freeze when I cannot follow a line of thought: when it will threaten my equilibrium.

In my dream a monster is chasing me. I run stumbling down a path. I can hear my heart beating and look down at my feet which will not go fast enough. I glance over my shoulder and see the monster moving with effortless strides closer and closer towards me. Now all I can hear is the thumping of my heart and I stumble and fall. Time stands still. I am motionless, frozen. The monster takes the last pace, reaches down

and I awake, sweating and shaking.

This is a common dreaming experience, when fear renders us immobile, rooted to the spot, speechless, dumb. We often describe this in terms of cold:

> Suddenly I was frozen, I could not move.
> My blood ran cold with fear.
> I felt myself freeze up when she began to speak.

When something happens in a dream that is so frightening that we freeze, we have one option left: we wake up, our release. The 'worst possible' is about to happen and we protect ourselves from it happening. In a dream we have created this phantom and ultimately we have the power to destroy it too. On waking, it becomes a mirage, half-glimpsed and then, thankfully, we turn away from it.

To be frozen also describes a waking state, an absence of emotion. To be frozen, to be numb: I can no longer feel. If I felt this emotion it would overwhelm me, therefore I block it out. Avoid it. Numb myself.

Polar explorers have often experienced an irresistible desire to go to sleep in the snow. If they give way, then the instinct for self-preservation is lost and death becomes inevitable.

It is easier to be numb and 'cold' than to be responsive and 'warm' when the stimulus is so threatening. To lie down in the snow and refuse to move any further: this is the anaesthesia when the struggle for life is given up. It no longer matters, the only thing that matters is to lie down, to sleep, to be invulnerable, to freeze.

Being frozen indicates a certain blindness – a voluntary turning away. I choose not to look at this, to be implicated, to be threatened, and so I will keep myself as still as possible, until I cannot move and am turned to ice. Then I will be motionless and passive. I will not be responsible.

It is far easier not to have certain thoughts.

It's estimated that in a nuclear war, in 30 days 90 per cent of Americans would be dead. Now I cannot accept that. Apparently there are some people who say, 'well, it's going to happen.' They've lost their most primitive, most powerful instinct, and that is for survival. So they are sick. But unfortunately it's become a collective psychosis in a way, because we all practice psychic numbing, and push it back here . . . We go to work . . . and we have the babies and we cook the cakes, and pretend it's going on forever. But you know that what I've said is true. We are all children of the atomic age, and somehow we've become passive. We are all responsible. This is the most serious medical issue ever to face the human race.

Well, what choice is there? Do I just go along and be a hedonist

and enjoy myself and practise medicine? When my kids are going to be blown up? Knowing what I know, what else can I do? What am I here for? Am I here just to enjoy myself? . . . We are the curators of every organism on this earth. We hold it in the palm of our hands, and this is the ultimate in preventive medicine: to eliminate every single nuclear weapon on earth, and close the reactors at once. For if we do not, we are participating in our own suicide.
Dr Helen Caldicott, *Critical Mass*

The most disturbing aspect of dreams about nuclear war is the way they relate to the very real threat of destruction that hangs not simply over our own lives, but over the future.

The effects of nuclear weapons lie in our heads as well as in radioactive fallout. The damage that is being done *now* to people's vision of the future and their faith in future generations is incalculable.

Personal responsibility

I've got two young children, and I've taken responsibility for their passage into adulthood. Everyone tells me they are my responsibility. The government tells me this. It is my responsibility to create a world fit for them to grow up in. I can't say I'm responsible for my children not catching whooping cough and *not* responsible for doing anything about the threat of annihilation which hangs over them every minute of the day. There were two things that really brought this home to me. I took my daughter to London Zoo one day as a birthday treat. Where we live in Wales it's very quiet. Every plane that went overhead frightened her, and she put her hands over her head saying, 'Mummy they're going to bomb us.' Suddenly I became really conscious that they *could* be: that's about as much warning as we would get. It seemed terrible that I was allowing her to grow up with this fear. I was forced to think about it, but then put it to the back of my mind again. Some time later, when I was about seven and a half months pregnant, I watched *Horizon*, about the 'Protect and Survive' plans. We in Wales would not be hit directly, and it became very plain to me that I would have to sit and watch my children die. Children are much more susceptible

to radiation than adults, and I would have to watch them die in
agony and then die myself. Suddenly it became obvious to me
that I had to do something for my children.
Susan Lamb, 1983

We might be frightened simply of thinking about nuclear
weapons at all and what they mean. The horror is so awful we push
it to the back of our minds. Thinking about them means we will
have to ask ourselves difficult questions, perhaps recognising that
our sense of security may be misplaced, that the future we plan and
save for, the home we live in, the friends and families we love are all
at risk and no security at all. For each woman associated with
Greenham and the thousands who identify with it, the necessity for
taking personal responsibility has grown out of feelings of anger
and desperation.

As Helen Caldicott says, 'We are the curators of every organism on this earth.' This means that we are *all* responsible for the
preservation of life. If we do not take up this responsibility we are
likely to destroy the world. This is a difficult idea to accept, for we
are not used to defining responsibility so broadly. Many women are
saying we must take a fundamentally different attitude, one which
encourages rather than denies individual responsibility, which
acknowledges the connection between caring for each other and
caring for the planet. No one will change this disastrous course for
us, we must do it ourselves – by proving that there are other ways of
organising, which do not depend on violence; by pointing out that
relying on threats and violence threatens life itself; by acknowledging that each person is responsible in their own way for the world in
which we live.

I used to wake in the middle of the night in a complete panic,
having dreamt the nuclear nightmare, the post-holocaust
dream. I was tired of this fear being thrust upon me. I felt I had to
do something and not just build a bunker in my back garden! I'd
heard of near catastrophes through computer error, through
mismanagement, through negligence, and was appalled at the
planning and contemplation for mass murder that was going on
all around me.

When I heard about the women's peace camp initially, I
must have pushed the idea into the back of my mind, because I
felt that the sacrifices that needed to be taken in order to make

such a direct action were too great for someone like me with two small children and a seemingly secure, cosy world.

But one day I had a letter from a woman in the peace camp telling of the threat of eviction that the women here faced. What was needed was a strong physical presence of women and it was something I could do. So I packed my sleeping bag up and drove the 200 miles or whatever it is up to Greenham Common not knowing what on earth to expect. I'd never been to a peace camp before. I didn't really know what was going on here. But the warmth and the love that I was greeted with, the total absence of suspicion, was a fantastic feeling and I really felt that I'd made the right decision.

The camp itself is a permanent reminder to the government that there are many people who don't want to be part of the nuclear arms race. We're not just a bunch of women sitting around a base. We're speaking for thousands of people who don't want cruise missiles sited here. It seemed a strange kind of democracy to me that a decision could be taken without even parliament being consulted, let alone the public. I sensed this sick mentality all around me that was motivated not by the sacredness of life but by *fear* that was feeding the arms race. It seemed crazy to me that the government were pouring our precious energies, our resources, billions of pounds, into something that was for mass murder, instead of this money going towards our social services, our health and education.

But it's not just a question of costs and alternative military strategy. It's a moral question. There's really only one thing you need to ask yourself, and that is: would you pull the trigger? would you press the button? and if the answer is 'No', then you have to work with us and help this struggle for peace.

The peace camp's more than just a brave gesture of defiance. It's an experiment in nonviolent resistance, the taking of responsibility by ordinary people, not just for what's being done in our name, but for how we behave towards each other. It was certainly my instincts that brought me here – a deeply based conviction that nothing in the world is more important than peace and that what's going on over there, behind those gates, is evil and only adds to our peril.

We plan to take direct action this weekend. We want to blockade the base for 24 hours by chaining ourselves to the

Pam Isherwood

Decorating the perimeter fence, Greenham Common,
12 December 1982

**gates, and we face possible arrest and imprisonment. I've been
accused of being cruel and hard-hearted for leaving my children
behind, but it's exactly *for* my children that I'm doing this. In the
past, men have left home to go to war. Now women are leaving
home for peace.**

Sarah van Veen, March 1982

It is hard to accept that *each individual* is to blame for nuclear
weapons – ourselves, our families, our friends. Thousands
of people do not want them and genuinely feel the present situation
is not of their making. This year the government will spend
£16,000,000,000 or so on 'defence'. This works out at about £18 a

Jenny Matthews

Decorating the perimeter fence, Greenham Common,
12 December 1982

week for every family. The army, navy, air force, weapons manufacture and research are all paid for with our money, from income tax, VAT, tax on cigarettes and drink. Of course, not everyone has equal power to effect a change – most of us do not have the same power as a cabinet minister, for example – but we all have the power of refusal in our own lives. If the government makes decisions we do not like we can go along with them – however reluctantly – or we can stand out against them and make our opposition clear. If we do not stand out against nuclear weapons, then we are – however reluctantly – supporting them.

The implications of this line of reasoning are enormous and

different for everyone. They are also frightening. We may be frightened

of taking risks, not knowing what will happen to us,

of standing out by making a personal statement,

of being embarrassed in public,

of being arrested, punished, or having a police record,

of losing security, perhaps our jobs, or the respect of people we had thought were friends.

Probably every group of women who sit down to discuss nuclear weapons and what can be done about them find themselves talking about these issues. It is only by talking through such fears and seeing that others share them that they cease to be so monumental and become less of a block to taking action.

A fundamental principle of women's actions is that these personal issues are seen to be an integral part of the process, not an embarrassing diversion to be left at home and dealt with separately on our own. Crossing this barrier of silence and isolation is the first step in breaking the chain of powerlessness.

We are all responsible for opening up this issue, for making sure that cruise missiles are a subject for debate, instead of being quietly deployed all over Europe, which is what our governments intended. A majority of people in this country are now opposed to cruise missiles. Two years ago most people had not even heard of them.

On 12 December 1982, 30,000 women from all over Britain, as well as groups from Sweden, Holland, West Germany and Ireland, encircled the base at Greenham Common. In the weeks that followed, hundreds of local papers carried articles about women involved in the peace movement and letters expressing their views. Women were interviewed on local radio stations and invited to speak at meetings. People talked about the action at Greenham all over the country. There is now a chain of women's peace groups. In virtually every town, women are talking about what they can do to express their opposition to nuclear weapons in their own neighbourhood – for example, highlighting the existence of military establishments, the danger from nuclear power stations and nuclear waste, and the inadequacies of civil defence planning.

At present there are over a dozen long-term peace camps in Britain besides the women's peace camp at Greenham Common. Faslane and Holy Loch peace camps are outside nuclear submarine bases in Scotland. There are peace camps outside US Air Force bases at Upper Heyford, Oxfordshire; Lakenheath, Suffolk; Daws Hill, near High Wycombe; Molesworth, Cambridgeshire; Burtonwood near Warrington, and Wethersfield in Essex. Other camps are protesting at the activities of RAF bases – Lossiemouth in Scotland; Bishopcourt in Northern Ireland; and Naphill, near High Wycombe, as well as against the chemical and biological warfare research centre at Porton Down and the Royal Ordnance factory at Burghfield. These peace camps and others which will be set up in the future all need continual support – money, food, equipment, ideas and encouragement.

People are campaigning against nuclear weapons through their trades unions. Local government employees in many areas are refusing to take part in training for civil defence programmes, which they believe to be wholly inadequate. There are peace education projects in some schools, introducing children to co-operative rather than competitive games and ways of working. Some civil engineers are discussing whether or not they should be designing and building nuclear missile silos. Some doctors – and, indeed, the British Medical Association – are recognising the enormous devastation nuclear war would bring, and emphasising that the present medical services would be unable to cope with more than a tiny fraction of the casualties.

The government spent more on 'defence' last year than on either health or education, and more than double what it spent on housing. It made very serious cuts in public spending between 1979 and 1983, especially in social services and health care. The cuts in public spending in socially useful services and increases in defence spending are two sides of the same coin. There are now fewer places in hospitals or day-care centres for the elderly and the sick, which means that they have to be looked after at home, invariably by women. Other women are involved in campaigning for nurseries and playgroups, for better pay for public service workers, trying to keep hospitals open, getting repairs done to council houses, and so on. Indirectly this is also a campaign against nuclear weapons, against the sickening waste and mismanagement of money, skills and resources invested in the arms race.

As these examples show, everyone has a point of contact with this issue through the areas we live in, the work we do, or the taxes we pay. Compared with the scale of the problem, these initiatives may seem fairly insignificant. However, we all have a responsibility to speak out against the threat of nuclear weapons.

I'm here at Greenham Common where they're building silos for 96 cruise missiles. I want to be here every day to remind these people of what they're doing. They're just ordinary guys who need jobs. If I weren't here every day, they'd be able to do their jobs with that much greater ease. I'm hoping to encourage them to leave their jobs. With my sign I say 'Can you stop for a talk?' and I do mean a *talk*. I don't argue with these people. Once you start to argue nobody listens to each other any more. I talk to them about the men in Germany who built prison camps and gas chambers before the war, never dreaming that they would be used for such atrocities. They needed work and thought they were doing something their nation needed. These people need jobs, but cruise missiles are far, far worse than any gas chamber. Each cruise missile is the equivalent of 15 Hiroshimas, and there are four cruise missiles on each lorry. If America makes trouble anywhere in the world this will have to be knocked out. The devastation that would entail . . . I no longer consider what I may achieve. To me it's important that I express myself about these missiles, and if I can encourage people to leave their jobs then that's great. There are so many ways people can express themselves. If we all gain that little bit of confidence to find our voices and do things then there's a hope of things changing. There's millions of people who don't like what's going on in the world. We've got to find ways of expressing ourselves.
Fran De'Ath, March 1982

After the second attempt to evict the peace camp at Greenham in September 1982, workmen began to lay sewer pipes, part of the expansion needed to house all the extra personnel who would accompany the cruise missiles. Several men arrived on the first afternoon and, with the aid of a large mechanical digger, began to turn over the earth and started to dig trenches. Women gathered at the edges of the site in small groups and stood silently watching. Some talked to the workmen, asking them whether they had considered the consequences of their work, how they felt about preparing the ground for cruise missiles. At first some of the men laughed to each other at the women, but quite quickly all the laughter stopped. The workmen were unable to look the women in the eyes, they looked embarrassed as they continued their work. Some of the women sang to the workmen, songs about the consequences of nuclear weapons, about the bombing of Hiroshima. All

Pam Isherwood

Police support construction workers by
breaking the women's blockade of the base,
Greenham Common, 13 December 1982

the time they looked into the eyes of the workmen, often they cried. The next day the group of workmen was smaller. Several construction companies now find it difficult to hire men to work at Greenham Common. Unwilling to lose the contract, one of these companies has written to all its ex-employees, asking if they would like a job at Greenham.

Many trade unions have passed resolutions expressing their opposition to working in the arms industries, and yet there is often no alternative employment or the firms involved use non-union labour, which makes these votes meaningless. In addition, parts for cruise missiles are made in West Germany, the USA, Canada and the UK. The dozens of companies engaged in supplying parts for weapons systems and preparing sites to house them are firms with such household names as Bendix, Singer, Goodyear and Tarmac.

There are obviously economic reasons for these facts, but one important result is that no one group of workers can be said to be responsible for the manufacture of nuclear weapons. The workers who laid sewage pipes could easily ignore the implications of their work, because all they personally were doing was laying pipes. Incidents like this underline the need to confront individuals.

This is reiterated over and over again in conversations with the police, magistrates, workers, whenever people reply: 'It's not a question of whether I agree with you, I'm just doing my job.' People often see themselves – and are encouraged to see themselves – as simply part of a corporate mass, and feel that the part they play is insignificant. It is individuals who make the silos, and the component parts for cruise missiles, and individuals who drag women away to police cells.

Unlike bad housing conditions, hospital closures or unemployment, nuclear weapons may seem very abstract. We never see them. They are strictly guarded in prohibited places. As far as we know, cruise missiles are not here yet. They are being paid for and will be controlled by the US, which makes them even more remote. But this government's commitment to nuclear weapons is having an impact now. Nuclear weapons are killing people now. People all across the world are dying of starvation, malnutrition, dirty water, pollution. The resources that are invested in arms could so easily be used to create better ways of living. Confronting individuals with the consequences of their work is only part of the process. We must all take responsibility for forcing men and women to work in the arms industries or support them in any other way.

Taking responsibility does mean changing our lives, changing what we think is important, how we spend our time and money, and it is something that everyone can do in their own way, making their individual contribution.

Taking direct action

When we heard that the women from the march to Greenham Common had stayed there and set up a peace camp outside the main gate, we decided to let people know what was happening by mimicking their action: we decided to live on the streets at Porth Square, Rhondda Valley, Wales. The press should be getting information about nuclear weapons across to people, but it's obvious that other people have to do their job for them. We must cut across all the misinformation which, either by accident or design, we are given. On the first day at Porth Square we didn't know what to expect. But we were in the street, and quite soon people's curiosity got the better of them and they started reading our leaflets and talking to us, even if at first they thought of us as a loony bunch of women. We went carrying four flasks. By the end of the first day we had 25 flasks lined up that had been given us. A man across the street brought us a bottle of whisky; his wife had not let him go to sleep until he brought something to keep us warm. Old people and children were the first to respond to us being there. Several old people came up and blessed us, saying they'd lost brothers in the first world war, sons in the second, and thank God someone was doing something to stop there being another war which would kill us all. We went out of

desperation and we came away knowing we could do it, because of the response of people – the way they opened their minds and talked. Every night people would come and talk to us. Perhaps they wouldn't go to meetings, but they could easily approach an individual and talk about their fears and what they could do. We can't leave everything up to committees, we must take action for ourselves. Women are often intimidated by organisations like CND. They could identify with us and would come and talk. Local people were very supportive. The action started a chain of letters to papers, and opened up discussion. The fact that people knew us all reinforced this.
Susan Lamb, April 1983

In August 1981 a group of women, children and a few men, marched from Cardiff to Greenham Common in protest at NATO's decision to site cruise missiles at Greenham. Much of South Wales is within a 200-mile target area based on Greenham Common, and it was women living in Wales who initiated the march. Some stayed and set up the peace camp. Other women in Wales decided to take supportive action, telling people about the peace camp and the issue of cruise missiles.

More and more women are using nonviolent direct action to express their opposition to nuclear weapons, informing other people and also the authorities of their opinions. The actions described in this chapter illustrate several points, including how an action might be organised; the reactions of the public and the police; and what women involved in the action felt about doing it. Most of them are connected with the Greenham Common women's peace camp. A few took place at Greenham, while others were inspired by the peace camp or were organised by women associated with it. This is not because we think these actions are more important, but simply because we know about them. Some of the numerous and imaginative actions that have taken place all over Britain are mentioned at the end of the chapter to give a sense of the scope of nonviolent direct action.

The first large action initiated by Greenham women in London was the die-in outside the Stock Exchange on 7 June 1982, coinciding with President Reagan's visit. Helen John from Greenham spoke to a massive CND rally in Hyde Park the day before, and invited women present to participate in an action in London the next day:

'You're within the 200-mile area where these weapons are going to be put and that makes you not a defended area, but a target for certain. We're taking an action tomorrow. We're going to institute a die-in. That's a very simple thing to do – you just lie down and die, because that's exactly what's going to happen if these missiles come here.'

Many of the women who responded to this invitation had not been associated with Greenham before. However, it was clear to them that larger and larger demonstrations were not actually changing anything.

Groups of six or seven women met in Hyde Park to discuss the action, what we felt about participating, the legal consequences, and what each woman would do – who would actually 'die', hand out leaflets or act as observers and peacekeepers. By the end of the afternoon about 80 women had gone through this process. Many women had arrived knowing no one, and by the end had a strong sense of being included within a small and supportive group. Early the next morning, those who had decided to do the action met again in Jubilee Gardens, and the overall feeling was of strength and confidence mixed with varying degrees of apprehension. The police had gathered in large numbers in Jubilee Gardens and followed our small groups to the underground station.

The aim was to lie down and 'die' across five roads around the Stock Exchange, thus effectively blocking all traffic going through the City. The Stock Exchange – one of the world's financial centres – was chosen to highlight the connection between the vast sums of money spent on nuclear weapons and the consequences in human lives. The road each group of women would lie across had been decided beforehand, and when we arrived at the Stock Exchange, women quickly lay down. In each group there were women handing out leaflets and trying to talk to passing office workers, explaining why the action was taking place: that the women were lying down to symbolise the one million who would be killed instantly in a nuclear attack on London. It was an attempt to confront people going to work, doing their job, with the realities behind the nuclear threat.

Reactions of passers-by to this action were predominantly hostile. Most people resented their morning routine being disrupted in this unforeseen way. One man snatched a woman's bundle of leaflets, tore them up and proceeded to stamp on them.

Paula Allen

Die-in at the Stock Exchange, 7 June 1982

The leaflet read:

'In front of you are the dead bodies of women.

  Inside this building men are controlling the money which will make this a reality, by investing our money in the arms industries who in turn manipulate governments all over the world and create markets for the weapons of mass destruction to be purchased again with our money.

  President Reagan's presence here today is to ensure American nuclear missiles will be placed on our soil. This will lead to you lying dead.

  As women we wish to protect all life on this planet. We will not allow the war games, which allegedly protect some whilst killing others, and lead to nuclear war which will kill us all.'

Motorists shouted and swore at the women. It was hard for the leafleters to keep calm and keep talking. Some people, however, took the leaflets and showed support for what was happening.

The police, arriving on the scene rather late because their vans had been held up by the traffic jams, found the whole situation rather confusing. They stood about for some time, giving women conflicting stories: some were told they were arrested, others just dragged away. In the end nine women were arrested, seemingly at random. The police obviously believed that they should make some arrests, and it did not seem to matter whom they chose.

We had planned a time limit of 15 minutes on the action. As it happened, we had underestimated the scale of disruption that 70 well-organised women could create by peacefully lying down in London streets. Once the action was over, it was possible to quietly disperse back into the rush-hour crowds. We made our way back to Jubilee Gardens in small groups, because it was important to meet together afterwards to make contact with each other again and to learn how to be more effective in the future.

If one person on their way to work had suddenly made the connection between the money spent on arms and the deaths of millions, then the action had been a success.

As important as an action itself is the organising that goes on to make it successful. Because people only see the result, and the aspects the media judge to be significant, these other processes go unseen except by those involved. For this reason, many actions can sometimes seem hard to identify with. They also appear spontaneous when this is often far from the truth.

While many women who took part in the Stock Exchange action spontaneously decided to join after the CND rally, other women had been thinking about it for some time. A few women had the idea of taking direct action in London. They talked about it with others until a plan began to emerge. Someone went to check the roads around the Stock Exchange and leaflets were written and printed to hand out on the day. It was decided that the action would be publicly announced, but not its location, for fear that the police would be at the Stock Exchange in force and prevent it happening. Only one member of each group knew the precise location. Photographers were contacted who could be trusted not to inform the police, and independent film-makers arranged to film the action. The time limit of 15 minutes was set for the duration of the action so that a realistic expectation could be defined. Women were allocated to phone newspapers on the day with details of the action and how it had gone. All of this was in addition to the work that went on in the groups the day before.

For many women, taking the first step is the hardest. Perhaps isolated at home or at work, where personal fears are not discussed, it is difficult to know how to begin and vital to have some means of meeting others who share our opinions. Tamar Swade, who started Babies against the Bomb, put a card in a newsagent's window asking other mothers with small children to contact her. Other women's peace groups have started from an informal meeting at someone's house, often after watching Helen Caldicott's video,

Critical Mass. Other women may already be members of women's groups, church organisations, the Women's Institute or the Housewives Register.

A year ago I started a branch of the National Housewives Register and groups of us met in different women's houses on the Isle of Wight. Our meetings were democratic and discussed issues, they weren't about our domestic lives. We talked about nuclear weapons, and there was a lot of pressure within the group to invite a man from the county council who visited schools and talked to meetings about civil defence. There were about 25 of us at this meeting. He horrified me. He was so smooth, gentle, kind and reassuring, very clever. I was not involved in the peace movement but I knew he was lying. I sat for three days afterwards, frantic and terrified.

I'd joined CND six months before although I hadn't become involved really. I rang up the local branch and went to see *Critical Mass*, which stunned me. It was the week before 12 December 1982. We cancelled everything for Christmas. We were going to have a party on 11 December, but hired the local cinema instead and showed *Critical Mass* to about 120 people. Women who were involved in the Greenham Common women's peace camp came to talk to the meeting.

I went to Greenham the next day, stayed overnight and joined in the blockade on 13 December. I had never done anything like this before and I was amazed at how strong I felt.

The CND meetings I had gone to used to drive me beserk. So I rang up a friend on the other side of the island and we arranged a meeting. About 15 women turned up. Now, four and a half months later, there are six groups on the Isle of Wight. They are all small, but each week they grow.

After Christmas we didn't know what to do, but it was clear that we should talk to as many people as possible. We decided to arrange a press conference in London and show *Critical Mass*. We didn't know about press releases, and so we got 100 cards printed like party invitations saying the Women for Life on Earth are holding a press conference, and sent them to every paper and magazine. About 50 journalists turned up to the meeting in a room above a pub in Fleet Street, including the editor of the *Financial Times*. We did it to get to journalists as ordinary people, not so they would necessarily print articles. I wanted to get the message across to ordinary women though, who read women's magazines.

I couldn't speak for terror. All I said was 'hello' and turned the video on. Afterwards a very smart woman photographer wanted to take a photograph of me outside. She had a lot of make-up on and, when we got outside, she burst into tears, crying, 'What can I do about all of this?' All her make-up was running down her face. We talked for a while and I gave her a list of things she could do.

In February, when the court cases were going on in Newbury for the women arrested on New Year's Day at Greenham, we decided not to go to the court, because we knew there were going to be a lot of women there already in support. Instead, we hired a hall for our children and held a vigil outside the court house in the Isle of Wight. Women had never demonstrated like that before on the island. We dressed in black clothes and walked around the streets handing out leaflets, talking to people and explaining why we were demonstrating. We must have talked to 3,000 people that day. None of the leaflets were thrown on the pavements. Women read them, took them home, and many joined us in the street. When the evening came we decided to stay all night. We lit a brazier and hung our banner on the courthouse flagpole. People came to talk to us till 3 a.m., giving us fuel for the fire and hot food.

There was a CND meeting recently to discuss direct action. It was all very theoretical, people discussing it in the abstract. Then a hand went up at the back and a Scottish girl asked in a really quiet voice if you can take a baby into prison. She knows she's going to go to prison over this.

We're having a children's party on Sunday at Greenham which has been organised by the Isle of Wight women. Women will go on to the base with their children. I believe it's only when children are involved that things will start to change. People will see that it's for real. The lives of our children are threatened.
Sue Bolton, April 1983

All the components to make an action a success are invisible but necessary. Each in itself is straightforward, and most skills are easy to learn if there is an urgent reason to do so. Many women have not been in a position to pick up these skills and a great deal of ingenuity and imagination goes into learning them. It was probably because the women from the Isle of Wight had never written a press release before, and sent cards that looked like party invitations, that 50 Fleet Street journalists turned up in a lunch hour to watch a 40-minute video film on the medical effects of nuclear war. If standard press releases had been sent, they could easily have been thrown into a pile with the rest and ignored.

Many people, both detractors and supporters, commented on the good organisation for the actions at Greenham Common on 12 and 13 December 1982. Women connected with the peace camp had organised firewood, water supplies, food, toilets, car parks, road signs, creche, lawyers and so on. They had produced a booklet with a map of the base, details about facilities available, notes about nonviolence, legal information, songs, and a programme for the two days. Everyone who took part in the blockade on 13 December registered with a co-ordinating group and was briefed about the action. Some women had been meeting beforehand and a few groups had already taken direct action together. The majority had never done anything like it before. Women who did not know each other joined into groups. Each person had a role to play and was immediately involved. The legal implications of the blockade were discussed early on in small groups. Anyone who did not want to be arrested knew that she could take a supporting role or, if blockading, that she could move out of the way when cautioned by the police.

Where there is a clear task, like trying to blockade the base for a day or 'dying' outside the Stock Exchange for 15 minutes, and everyone takes responsibility for her part in the action, it is much more likely to succeed and to be a positive experience for those taking part. It is important to provide legal back-up and practical support as well as support for court cases and press coverage, so that everyone feels confident. Spontaneous actions without this practical back-up can lead to people becoming over-stretched and feeling that they are not being effective.

The care that goes into planning women's actions is vital, giving each woman a chance to learn the necessary skills, talking through possible consequences, taking the time to make sure that each woman is feeling confident and wants to take the action. There is always an understanding that each woman is responsible for herself, and that no one should feel pressured to act in a way that she feels uncomfortable with. This absence of 'bravado' means everyone is certain that they are doing what is right for them and not what someone else thinks they 'ought' to do.

gies. The police reaction to the blockade at Greenham on 13 December is a case in point:

> Police were instructed not to arrest the Greenham Common demonstrators yesterday, and instead moved hundreds bodily from the gates around the base.
>
> Many of the 2,000 protestors who stayed the night had slept across the 16 entrances on the 9-mile perimeter in their attempts to shut the base.
>
> All day the police and a nucleus of 700 activists had a tactical struggle to get the upper hand. At the end last night, only two women and a man had been arrested and all sides were claiming a success.
>
> Assistant Chief Constable Wyn Jones, who was in charge of the operation said: 'We have been very conscious that these are ordinary law-abiding women who believe passionately in their cause.'
>
> He said hundreds of women had committed arrestable offences during the day but they were not 'vindictive or malicious'.
>
> They were not the sort of women who would normally come to police attention and he did not expect them to do so again.
>
> 'They were demonstrating because of their deeply held political convictions,' he added. 'I do not think the circumstances justify the full sanctions of the criminal law.'
>
> (The *Guardian*, 14 December 1982)

It would be nice to be able to take these much publicised words of Wyn Jones at face value. However, in practice, it would have been very hard for the police to arrest such large numbers of women. Television cameras and press reporters made aggressive police tactics unwise. There was obviously great support for the women's action all over the country.

All this did not stop many isolated incidents of police harrassment and outright violence:

My impression was that the police were being reasonably restrained and some seemed to be sympathetic. One put me down very gently on the grass with an 'excuse me'! Another, obviously exasperated, pleaded with me not to go back on to the road . . . Some police, however, were far from gentle; perhaps understandably through sheer exasperation. Some, I felt from studying their facial expressions, were being deliberately violent. I was dragged once by the hood of my cagoule, which was across my throat, which meant I couldn't breathe; I tried to scream but couldn't, and from the violence with which I was thrown down at the side, I was still retching and choking. I am sure that was deliberate. Another time I was dragged by the hair, which was up

in a plait. Several women told me they had been kicked on the head and in the stomach, though I only saw one incident myself. A woman lay at my feet having her head kicked by a policeman, whose number was covered by a plastic mackintosh. She was screaming and crying and the women around her were screaming at the man to stop . . . An elderly Swedish woman to whom I spoke was in a lot of pain, very pale and weeping, because she thought her arm had been broken. Later examination proved that it had not, but it had been viciously twisted, she said deliberately. The woman next to me had her face kicked and her glasses broken. I was trying to catch a policeman's eye to prevent them from trampling her further, and also trying to protect her with my body . . . My impression remains that they were obviously under orders to be restrained and most of them were managing to be reasonably good-natured. Some were deliberately violent from the outset, and some were unnecessarily violent through sheer exasperation. They were obviously not used to dealing with totally nonviolent women and some over-reacted.
Helen Steven, 13 December 1982

How the police deal with our actions varies a lot, depending on circumstances and on individual police officers. We often find ourselves talking about how the police behave and many women are understandably nervous of them. It is the police we come up against, but they are not our 'target'. Nonviolent women's actions in this country have so far not encountered concerted violent reactions from police. Reactions to nonviolent direct actions elsewhere in Europe have not been so restrained.

In March 1983, a group of women from Greenham visited Comiso in Sicily. Magliocco airport near Comiso is due to receive 112 American cruise missiles. These will serve a dual purpose: because they could reach 800 miles further south than cruise missiles elsewhere in Europe, taking in Libya and Egypt, they could be used either in a European conflict or a conflict which developed in the Middle East.

In 1981, two-thirds of Comiso's population signed a petition calling for the cancellation of the decision to site cruise missiles there, arguing that as well as being against the will of the people, the Paris Peace Treaty of 1947 forbade the use of Sicily for military ends. A march to protest against the decision on 4 April 1982 attracted about 75,000 people, the largest demonstration in Sicily since the second world war. While local people are clearly not apathetic, there is a feeling that a decision taken by the Italian government will not be revoked, and local people are divided about Comiso being a focus for international attention.

A peace camp was set up outside Comiso in July 1982, as a permanent voice of protest, with supporters from Italy and the rest of Europe visiting and taking nonviolent direct actions to draw attention to the situation. In March 1983, women from Italy, England, Ireland, America, Holland, Germany, France and Switzerland, began a week of nonviolent actions beginning with the formation of a large circle outside the base on 8 March, International Women's Day. On 9 March, 40 women blockaded the main gate of the base and were subject to harrassment and increasing violence from the police. Women had their hair pulled out at the roots, they were thrown on to the side of the road on top of each other, and one woman's wrist was broken. On 11 March, 16 women blockaded the road. In the course of their action the violence became much worse and a woman from England had her wrist broken. Twelve women were arrested and taken to the prison at Comiso. They were later transferred to a nearby prison at Ragusa, and held in extremely bad conditions until their deportation on 17 March. After their arrest, everything belonging to the peace camp was taken by the police, and the remaining traces were burned.

The action taken by the women had been completely nonviolent at all times.

I found the whole experience of being at Comiso quite shattering. We held a meeting the evening after the trial of the women who had been arrested should have taken place. It didn't, because the women were deported instead. It was a mixed meeting, but it was agreed that the men would let the women speak, which they did, and what was said was very moving and powerful. I was glad that the men heard that. Someone asked me in what way my experiences in Sicily were different from my experiences in England. Obviously, people had the violence in mind. I said I thought that it was part of a continuum: it wasn't different in kind, just different in degree. The Italian police had swept out the peace camp, destroyed it and then burned it. There were about four days of vindictiveness and quite extraordinary violence. All because 16 women lay down in a road. Someone remarked that in England they were using the process

Raissa Page

Women dancing on a missile silo, Greenham Common,
1 January 1983

of the law to get rid of the peace camp, whereas in Italy the police just marched in and destroyed the whole place, and then put everything that was left in a pile and burned it.

I felt that the end result was the same – the destruction of the peace camp. One went through the process of law and one didn't, but both were attacks on the peace movement . . .

Martha Street, April 1983

There are occasions when arrests have led to imprisonment in this country – when women charged with a breach of the 'peace' have refused to agree to be bound over to 'keep the peace', and when those arrested for obstruction refused to pay the fine. Direct action around a military establishment could lead to offences under the Official Secrets Act, which carry much harsher sentences.

Some women wanted to go on to the base on New Year's Day, on to the silos, to show their determined opposition to cruise missiles and to draw attention to the fact that the silos were already well under construction. In the event they were charged with a breach of the peace. It is easy to overlook the fact that the women involved were all aware that they risked very much more serious charges. The decision to take part in such an action, or to go to prison rather than agree to be bound over, is obviously not undertaken lightly – this was no New Year's party stunt.

As soon as we arrived at the camp a woman came down the path towards us and asked us if we'd heard the plan – to go on to the base at dawn and on to the silos, using ladders and carpets for the barbed wire! We were all amazed; it was such an incredible plan! I immediately felt really strongly that I wanted to do it. I had to try hard to hold back, to think about it rationally. We were worried about being charged under the Official Secrets Act.

But I knew my feelings about it would win over and that I'd end up going over the fence. It was because it was all centred around those missile silos. I think they're a focal point of all the negative things that are going on in the world – paranoia, greed, misuse of power, violence, a lack of imagination for alternatives. In my mind I saw them as revolting man-made boils on the earth's surface, full of evil. I wanted to let out all the feelings I have about the threat of nuclear war – the fear and the dread. And I wanted to concentrate on the future, to feel optimistic and get strength and hope that we can stop it. I kept thinking about celebrating life. What actually happened was that I did that. When we got on to the silos, even though we were so excited, I stood quietly for a few minutes, with my eyes closed, and let it all drain out of me. After that I just kept thinking about being alive!

There were about 60 of us at the last planning meeting, all quite calm, but there was a nervousness in the air. The next morning it was very still and dark outside as we crept into the back of the van. The journey to the base seemed endless. I was leaning forward looking out of the window, so I could see when we arrived. The only thing I could make out in the back of the van were the white women-signs painted on the tabards we were wearing so that we wouldn't be mistaken for terrorists, to make it obvious who we were.

The atmosphere was electric when we got to the base. We got out of the van as quietly and quickly as we could and immediately made our way to the perimeter fence. By the time we got there the first lot of women were going over, and half of them were already waiting on the other side.

Ahead of us we saw the aluminium ladders. I remember seeing three on each side, leaning against the fence. It seemed ridiculously easy – there were streams of women going over the fence, over the carpet, making it so ineffectual. There was a queue to get over. Just then we saw vehicle headlamps in the distance coming towards us. My heart sank. We knew we'd been seen, and wondered whether we'd manage to get over in time. It turned out to be a small vehicle with only two police inside.

I was on the ladder, about to go over, I was on the carpet . . . They whipped the ladders away and I was left stranded on the top wondering how I was going to get down. I scrambled over the wire at the top, jumped down, and then I put the ladder back up. The two police were running from side to side with their arms out, backwards and forwards, saying 'Stop, go back' – as if we'd all stop and go back. I remember deliberately running wide in a curve to avoid them, and running like hell. I remember getting there and scrambling up the slope. It was covered in mud and very slippery. At the top there was a big ledge of concrete we had to climb on to. A woman leaned down to offer me a hand up. I said, 'Hang on a minute, I can't manage just yet.' I had to get my breath back, I was really puffing. I climbed up that last bit of concrete and felt really pleased – I'd got there!

Every now and again we'd link arms in a big circle and dance around the top of the silo. We were all ecstatic, overtaken by the brilliant feeling that we'd actually done it! We took off our tabards and hung them on wooden posts to leave some trace and to remind the workmen that we'd been there, to make them think about it, and we planted a lovely colourful 'Peace 83' banner on the sloping side. The top of the silo was covered in bits of concrete rubble and wooden planks which we arranged into women's peace signs. When we began to explore the top of the silo we could see that we were only on one half of it. In between the two halves there was a deep rectangular pit with lots of steel reinforcing bars running across it like a grid. I suppose they were going to concrete it over. We went over to the far end and we could see the enormous airstrip. It looked really desolate. You could see for miles. There was nothing – just a watery sun coming up.

We were on top of the silos for about one hour and 20 minutes. A police car or two arrived first, then quite a bit later the buses arrived. I don't think they could believe how many of us there were. There we were on the top, celebrating New Year! The police walked around the bottom of the silo for quite a while, looking puzzled. Then some MoD police arrived and some military personnel.

When we saw the MoD police climbing up the side of the silo we all sat down around the edge of the big wooden peace sign, linked arms and just waited. They broke the circle and started lifting women down one by one. The police on the top picked up the women and passed them to the ones further down who dragged the women down the slope. One of the ones on the top was really nasty, much bigger than the rest, and he looked really threatening. I hoped he wouldn't be the one to get me. When they took a woman from the circle we all linked arms again and moved inwards, so the circle got smaller and smaller. The atmosphere changed but all the time we were friendly to the police.

One came to get me, and I went limp. He dragged me to the ledge and passed me over to two others, placing me on the ground on my front. I had my head facing down the slope . . . it was quite steep . . . They picked me up by the wrists and somehow my arms were pulled backwards as they dragged me. I thought they'd dislocate my shoulders. It was really painful. They said 'Get up and walk, you silly bitch. Are you going to get up and walk?' I was carried like that for about 20 yards or so. It was so painful I just said 'Please, put me down. I'll walk.' So they put me down and I walked. For the rest of the weekend I was extremely stiff and under my arms felt very bruised.

I had a conversation with one of the police near the bus. The other one had gone off again to get someone else. I said, 'Why don't you think about what you're doing? Don't you ever think about what you're protecting here?' I was just met with stony-faced silence. I gave up and just sighed and said, 'How will we ever get through to you?' He said, 'You don't realise, you already have, but this time you've overstepped the mark.'

We were all whisked off to Newbury nick, singing all the way. When we arrived we were taken down to the cells in the basement and put into a small room, which was the biggest cell they'd got. The noise of our singing was deafening. The police seemed to be affected in the same way as the base personnel – completely awestruck that we'd done it and that we were so jubilant about it.

We'd asked on the bus what we were being charged with and they said breach of the peace which was a big relief! They spent the whole day processing us. We were taken to a little room at the end where there were two police. One read out the charge sheet and took down particulars – names and addresses. Afterwards we were put into different cells, smaller, like pens. There were little bits of paper stuck to the walls outside with our surnames listed – the kind of thing that if we hadn't been feeling so good we'd probably have felt really angry about. We kept asking where we'd be taken to. They either didn't know or they wouldn't tell us.

Our cell door was opened. I was called out and put into another cell down the corridor. It was a different kind of cell, with no bench, just a loo with no chain. The chain was on the outside, I suppose so they can check what goes down the loo. It felt horrible in that cell by myself.

We heard the cell doors being unlocked. We were let out and led outside. There was a riot van waiting, with cages like tiny cupboards with a grid, all painted white. We were told that we were going to Oxford. Two of the women had to sit in a tiny space in the middle between the cages, and they had their wrists handcuffed together behind their backs. I felt very frightened, and horrified that we were going to travel all that distance in such a confined space, locked in, with our hands handcuffed like that.

All of a sudden I realised how barbaric it was and that I didn't have to do it. They got one handcuff on my left arm and they kept trying to grab my right arm to get the other handcuff on it, while I waved my right arm about so that they couldn't grab it. I was determined not to be handcuffed. I said that we weren't going to get away, that I'd deliberately put myself in this position and that we weren't going to escape with police in the van and the doors locked. The more I went on the more determined I became and the more frightened. I said 'What if there's an accident? How on earth are we going to protect ourselves?' They kept telling me not to argue. I thought that sooner or later I'd have to give in to their authority, but then I thought, just because they're police in uniforms I don't have to do it. They were shouting by this stage and I was shouting back, 'You don't have to do this. It's not necessary. It's just spite and humiliation.' Finally they gave in. They let the other women out and took their handcuffs off and handcuffed us to each other in a line. I was on the end so I had a free hand. I remember feeling so relieved.

Juliet Nelson, May 1983

Most nonviolent direct actions do not lead to arrests or imprisonment, nor do they need to do so to make their point. On 8 March 1983, International Women's Day, about 7,000 women from all over Western Europe and from America and Asia demonstrated against cruise and Pershing missiles in Brussels. In London, a group of women handed out 'peace pies' outside the Bank of England at lunchtime. They had posters saying 'Bread not Bombs' to make the connection between the squandering of vast resources on weapons, and famine and malnutrition, especially in the Third World. Women brought cakes, each with a message about peace, either pinned to the cakes like little flags or tucked under them. This action had a pleasant, gentle atmosphere. It is unusual to be given something nice by a stranger in the street, and it generated constructive conversations about peace and disarmament with the people who passed by. One woman, dressed as a waitress, offered a cruise missile to passing businessmen. But it turned out that none of them had ordered it!

Passing on information is a vital part of nonviolent direct action. Many people are involved in preparing leaflets, displaying posters, organising film shows and discussions. Brighton women's

peace group started a women's peace magazine, *Lysistrata*. A simple way of passing on information is to leave leaflets in library books, telephone boxes, on the counter in the post office or bank, in doctors' waiting rooms, or public toilets. Another way is through graffiti, especially drawing attention to military buildings, from bunkers to Territorial Army headquarters; or leaving messages in other public places, especially where people wait.

Women have collected signatures in support of the women at the peace camp, and expressing their opposition to cruise missiles. They have then sent these petitions to MPs or to the prime minister. Others have written letters to local papers, taken part in phone-in programmes on local radio, and done interviews for local radio stations. Many have been involved in demonstrations in their own town, or in vigils and pickets outside military establishments or outside courts, police stations or prisons, where other women are being held.

There have been several marches which have led to other actions. The Copenhagen-to-Paris peace march in the summer of 1981 directly inspired the Women for Life on Earth peace march from Cardiff to Greenham Common, and at the beginning of June 1982, from Cardiff to Brawdy in Pembrokeshire, the largest US submarine tracking station in Europe. Like the die-in at the Stock Exchange, this march coincided with Reagan's visit to Britain.

In the summer of 1982 there was a march in London organised by Babies against the Bomb. The whole procession was led by women in black mourning dresses, with push chairs, empty except for a 'tombstone' placard with the name of a child killed in Hiroshima or Nagasaki. During the Falklands War, women in Sheffield occupied the army recruiting office for a day, as a protest against the use of violence to resolve conflicts. On 12 October 1982, the day of the Falklands 'victory' parade in London, a group of women turned their backs as the parade passed them, symbolising their rejection of war.

In February 1983, women decorated the railings along the North London railway line with children's toys and clothes. This made a direct connection between the base at Greenham, decorated on 12 December, and the North London line, which regularly carries nuclear waste for reprocessing at Windscale in Cumbria. The waste trains travel at about 3 a.m., so that many people do not know that such lethal material is being transported through the middle of this densely populated area.

Women are campaigning against war toys, writing to manufacturers and politicians, and demonstrating outside shops. Two women from Yorkshire sent Mother's Day cards to Margaret Thatcher, as a reminder of her responsibility for their children's future.

Brighton women set up a peace camp on common land in the middle of the town. It started in the middle of February, when the women who had been arrested on the silo at Greenham started their prison sentences. Instead of lasting 14 days, as originally planned, the peace camp was very well supported for two months and provided an opportunity for many women to get to know each other and to plan other activities. Similarly, people in Sheffield squatted a disused building in the city centre and used it as a peace centre for several months. The city council had been promising to provide a permanent peace centre for a couple of years and they agreed to leave this building on the condition that this promise would be honoured.

On 17 January 1983 about 200 women went to the Houses of Parliament to tell MPs directly about their opposition to cruise missiles. Some made sure that their opinions reached the ears of other MPs by sitting down inside the House of Commons, where they were detained for several hours before being allowed to go. On 20 April 1983, a group from Brighton went into the Public Gallery during a debate about holding a referendum over cruise missiles. Most MPs voted against the proposal, but the women took the opportunity to remind them of Mrs Thatcher's famous remark at the time of the Falklands War – 'The wishes of the islanders are paramount' – before being forcibly removed from the gallery.

This is necessarily a cursory list because numerous actions have happened over the past months. The strength and scope of this growing network was clear on 24 May, International Women's Day for Disarmament. This day was first celebrated in 1982 with 90 events all over the country and several events in other countries, notably the establishment of a women's peace camp at Soesterberg in Holland.

Remarkably little media coverage was given to the widespread action on 24 May 1983, despite press releases, interviews with journalists and television crews filming actions all day. Carrie Pester was one of the women involved in coordinating news of the actions.

GLC peace bus, Camden Town, London, International Women's Day for Disarmament, 24 May 1983

The day was a phenomenal success, involving several hundred thousand women in Britain alone. In every city, town, and most villages, women were saying no to nuclear weapons and informing others on the issue. Die-ins were held in many towns; women

encircled, invaded, and blockaded bases, communications centres and army recruitment centres; and they drew attention to local nuclear bunkers and areas designated as mass burial sites in the event of war. In Peckham, South London, crosses were hammered into the ground planned for a mass graveyard. In Plymouth, 500 women blockaded the entrance to the naval base and later staged a die-in in the city centre. Over 100 women in Hexham, Yorkshire, picnicked on their local nuclear bunker and then formed a chain to the nearby abbey. The events of the day are far too numerous to list. All the actions were organised on a local level by women's peace groups up and down the country, and, put together, they demonstrated an unprecedented commitment on the part of women everywhere to take action for peace.

Internationally, at least 20 separate actions took place in Connecticut, USA. We had reports of other USA actions in Washington, Philadelphia, Pennsylvania, Florida, Montana, Boston and Northampton. In New Zealand, another 20 actions took place, including 1,000 women in Wellington and 20,000 in Auckland. Other countries that contacted us about actions were Australia, Switzerland, France, West Germany, Sweden, Denmark, Norway, Italy, Eire and Zimbabwe. We even received a telex of support from Costa Rica. The knowledge that we are an international force gives us strength. Hundreds of thousands of people must have been utterly astonished at the lack of coverage of an event that had touched millions of lives.

Of course, national news headlines were not the main aim of the day. It was another opportunity for women everywhere to replace their fear with action, and for those who had taken action before to encourage those who hadn't. All the women who took part on 24 May will talk to their friends and neighbours and fellow trade unionists who will join them next time.

The women's peace movement is unstoppable. The lack of media recognition merely confirms the established interest's fear of that force. As a friend remarked, 'Which other country springs to mind where we are told dissent is not reported?'
Carrie Pester, May 1983

Nonviolence

'Since I've been taking action at Greenham I've encountered all kinds of violence, from the abuse and sometimes blows of individual police to the institutional violence of the legal and prison systems. On their scale, using their rules, I am powerless. If I try to use their means they will always manage to harm me more than I can dent them. I wouldn't be taking action like entering the high security area of the base and dancing on the half-built cruise missile silos as we did on New Year's Day if I didn't feel frightened and angry about what they are doing. But my anger and fear have to be channelled into creative opposition. Sometimes it's incredibly hard to lie down and sing as I am being manhandled by the police or sentenced to 14 days in prison. But every time that happens, 10 or 100 more women realise that they have been passive too long and start taking responsibility themselves for protecting life against the nuclear threat.'
Rebecca Johnson, May 1983

All the actions described in the last chapter recognise the validity of personal experience, feelings and ideas. They involve starting where we are now and building on what we can do, so that we

63

Ed Barber

define our own course of action for our own reasons. They are all public statements, bearing witness to beliefs and drawing public attention to the issue in a very direct way, whether they involve a few women handing out leaflets in the street and talking to passersby, or 30,000 women forming a massive circle around the base at Greenham on 12 December 1982 and decorating the fence with personal belongings connected to real life.

Beyond this, the actions exemplify several important principles fundamental to nonviolence. They involve making contact with people, trying to generate discussion, not arguments that simply antagonise and alienate. If people are drawn into a conversation they are much more likely to be convinced by what we are saying and to support the action in some way. If they are hostile to begin with they can only change their minds if they are given the opportunity, if what people are saying seems reasonable. The women at Porth Square in Wales felt that one reason why their action was successful was that many people knew them already and felt able to talk to them as individuals, whereas they did not make contact with established organisations like CND. Handing out 'peace pies' outside the Bank of England was another way of opening up conversation with passers-by. More indirectly, going on to the silos drew people's attention to the fact that the silos are under construction, that they actually exist. Many actions try to make connections between things that may seem separate: for example, highlighting the vast resources invested in arms while famine kills so many people, simply because money is spent on warfare rather than the necessities of life.

Keening actions try to make contact with people on a different level, touching them emotionally, without the use of words.

We went to the Houses of Parliament to keen on 18 January 1982 because this was the day that the politicians came back from the Christmas recess. We wanted to say right at the very beginning of the parliamentary year, 'It's enough. We've had enough.' Keening is something done traditionally by women and is now confined to mourning. It's a means of expression without words, without having to get tied up in various arguments, facts and figures, whys and wherefores. You can just show how you feel. At the camp at Greenham we've always had a nonviolent approach to protest. We felt that this was a nonviolent way of expressing our feelings to our representatives in parliament, who should take account of the people they represent. Had we just gone there and stood outside with a banner we could easily have been ignored, but by using sound we could actually penetrate the building. We didn't want to just shout slogans. Politicians are hardened to this sort of thing. They've had it said to them so many times by so many people that it doesn't touch them anymore. We made trees of life. We covered twigs with ribbons in suffragette colours – purple, green and white – and hung doves of peace from them and little sequins. We made them beautiful things. Our banner said:

> **Our hearts are breaking. Politicians, you must rethink nuclear policy in 1982.**

Nuclear weapons now exist and they seem to reflect the state that society is in – our expectations, our values, our priorities are just so *wrong*. It's difficult to think how to change things, but to show your feelings is a very good way of beginning.
Jayne Burton, March 1982

Confrontation is a central part of nonviolence, but confrontation without recourse to violence or aggression.

Confrontation: to meet face to face, stand facing; be opposite to; face in hostility or defiance; oppose; bring (person) face to face with (accusers . . .)

Claire Hershman

2,000 women take nonviolent direct action
by blockading the base, Greenham Common,
13 December 1982

This dictionary definition stresses the active part of confrontation. It is about stating opposition clearly, standing face to face. If we make use of the threat of violence in direct action, then we do not truly oppose, we are not opposite, because we are using aggression to oppose aggression. We confront by making connection, and by drawing attention to our real situation in a society working towards self destruction.

Military planners merely regard us as collateral damage. The fact that millions of people will die hideous deaths does not prevent the planning for nuclear war, nor the government's acceptance that a nuclear 'exchange' would be the 'answer' to international conflicts. If we use violence against this sickness, we mask the true nature of the situation. We do not possess the weapons of coercion and see no solution in possessing them. We must work in a different way and use confrontation to express our opposition in many imaginative ways.

Demonstrations are the most common way to show opposition but the strength or weakness of a demonstration is judged in numbers: many thousands and the demonstration is considered a success, only a few hundred and it has failed. Demonstrations tend to keep opposition within a static framework of 'acceptable' protest. We need to produce a change in consciousness, a questioning of violence as a valid option, opening up channels of debate. Nonviolence is not concerned with numbers primarily, but with creating a situation in which different options and responses can be explored.

The die-in outside the Stock Exchange in June 1982 made a clear connection between what weapons do, and people making money out of the arms race, challenging people who work in the City of London to think about their involvement in a system which makes money out of war and killing. Blockades at Greenham confront the police, who protect the base, with the reality of what they are protecting, and the construction workers with the reality of what they are building. This is very provocative in a way that an angry mob can never be, because it is easy to shut off from or deride shouted slogans. The use of aggression reduces people's options to two absurdities: complete acceptance or complete rejection. There is no room for questioning because no attempt has been made to reach us, and we are immediately excluded. There is no debate for us to become involved in.

The police and the courts expect violence to be the inevitable result of confrontation. Women have been arrested for 'behaviour likely to cause a breach of the peace' on several occasions after taking nonviolent direct action. Breach of the peace means potential violence; it implies that had the police not intervened and arrested the women, violence would have occurred. Equating confrontation with potential violence artises from a deeply embedded assumption that violence is innate or inevitable. People assume that violence is a central part of human nature, or that because there has always been violence there always will be. People venerate cultures based on hierarchical principles that resort to violence to solve conflicts. Many people believe violence to be an inherent part of close involvement with other people. To step back and begin to question this assumption means that some deeply held beliefs are turned on their heads. Nonviolent confrontation assumes that nonviolence is at least as accessible (if not more accessible) a part of human nature as violence is.

It is important to differentiate anger and violence, whereas many people equate the two. Anger does not inevitably lead to, or express itself in, violence, and yet people often assume it does. When taking nonviolent action, your very vulnerability is your strength. For example, having put yourself in a position of apparent weakness by lying in the road, you trust that the motorists in the City or the truck drivers at Greenham will not run over you, and that the police will not beat you or kick you.

We must constantly put the responsibility for the use of violence back in the hands of the authorities, and this is only possible if we completely disown violence ourselves.

I've been quite badly bruised by the police, but they are accessible . . . just looking at them and saying 'This is my body. I'm protecting my life with my body because I don't feel protected by you and these weapons. Why are you trying to harm me? Why are you so threatened by me? Aren't you more threatened by cruise missiles?' I've not found a policeman able to use violence after that.

Rebecca Johnson, May 1983

By going limp on arrest we force the police to move us. They have to take the initiative and responsibility for doing this against our will and without our co-operation. Clearly, in confrontations with the police there is scope for very different responses. The police often discuss the use of violence as something forced upon them to deal with an otherwise uncontrollable situation. When dealing with nonviolent women's actions, the choice is firmly in their hands. If they choose to use outright violence to deal with a nonviolent situation, the nature of their intervention becomes very clear. It is important to recognise that the police always have violence as an option, just as everyone has a choice to accept or reject the build up of nuclear weapons.

In all the actions described in the previous chapter, the aims are to make a strong and clear statement. This runs from each woman's conviction, through the means employed to make that statement, taking the action, to dealing with its immediate consequences. Using nonviolence as a process and a way of thinking, as well as a strategy for action, means it is more likely that the integrity of all these aspects will be maintained. This rests on the assumption that collectively as well as individually we can take control of a situation and define our own boundaries. We can never know exactly how others will respond to us, but we can maintain clarity over how we shall behave towards them. We make a decision to screen out various things which, normally, we would pay attention to. Feelings of fear, nervousness or anger have been considered and, temporarily, put on one side, so that there is a unity of thought and feeling that is very strong and clear.

As women, we are particularly used to responding to situations rather than defining them from the outset. In taking nonviolent action we set up the situation on our own terms and keep the initiative by not allowing ourselves to be deflected by attempts to undermine that resolve. Nonviolence, far from being weak, actually feels very strong to participate in.

This is brought out in the following account of the first blockade of the base at Greenham Common. It involved about 200 women and lasted for 24 hours, starting at 6.30 p.m. on Sunday, 21 March 1982, the spring equinox. On the Monday morning the people who usually work on the base wanted to get in to go to work. Instead of moving the women at the gates, the police opened up a gap in the perimeter fence, in effect creating a new gate which they controlled. When women heard about this gap groups volunteered to come round from the other gates to blockade here. The first two groups were arrested but the police must have decided that was pointless as more and more women were arriving at the gap. So they stopped arresting and pulled the women away from time to time to let the vehicles through.

For the last half-hour from 6 to 6.30 all the women who were there sat down in front of the gap. Before that we'd been doing it in shifts. We were pretty tired and bruised but our spirits were still high. When it came to 6.30 an inspector came over to the police and said, 'OK, lads, that's it' and they shuffled off in orderly rows. We leapt up. I can only say we had a sort of celebration. We hugged and kissed each other and felt wonderful. It was extraordinary. We felt as if we'd won a victory in a way – a moral victory. Somehow we found ourselves in this enormous circle. I don't know how many of us there were. There were enough to make a really big circle that took up the whole of the road, right from the base fence across to the other side of the road. We took up the whole of the space, dancing and singing for a while. It was lovely. Then one woman suggested that we should stand in silence to calm ourselves down. So we all stood in this enormous circle, smiling in silence for a few minutes. It seemed quite a long time. It was very restful and calming and we felt very close to each other.

The police had all gathered over by the van that was going to take them away. They'd been joking and laughing but they fell silent. They just stood there looking at us. I don't know whether they understood what our celebration and quietness was about, but it made them speechless. All the time we were silent they didn't move, they didn't speak. It showed them, I think, that what they'd done hadn't touched us in any way. We were still as strong then as we were at the beginning. All the hauling about they'd done, all the carrying us off, hadn't come anywhere near to affecting our determination to go on doing what we'd been doing. Then we broke the circle. There was more hugging and kissing and laughing, and then we broke into groups and walked back to the camp.

Lesley Boulton, March 1982

These feelings of strength are an important contrast to many people's view of nonviolence as passive, reactive and weak. It is important to differentiate between the surface appearance – women lying down in the road, or being dragged by the police – and the underlying reason for it. Some people take issue with what they see to be passive, 'feminine' behaviour, self-denigrating and subservient, which is not at all what the women involved in the actions feel. Though you appear to be surrendering your body, you

Climbing into the base, Greenham Common,
1 January 1983

are in complete control. You make a conscious decision to take
part; you take the initiative and create the situation; and you can
choose to leave. This is very different from other kinds of demonstrations where confrontation is very often out of control. People

jostle and scream at the police, are nervous and off-balance.

This feeling of calm and centredness leads to situations where we can do far more than we ever thought possible. Preparation before the action, and consensus decision-making are also vital in achieving this. Nonviolence should run through everything we do from the details of an action, the process of deciding these details, and how we behave towards each other. For example, women who planned to go on to the base at Greenham on New Year's Day decided not to cut the fence or damage it in any way, but to use ladders to climb over it, and to cover the barbed wire with layers of carpet, thus 'softening' and neutralising it. This decision was not made by a leader or committee but by those taking part on a consensus basis.

In this society we are most used to majority decision-making, which is not the same thing at all. In majority decision-making, a situation is defined to start with as a choice between a limited number of options. These options are framed as two or three competing points of view and everyone chooses between them. This leads to a situation where the person who puts the most forceful argument often dominates, and the options become polarised and fixed. It assumes that it is possible and sensible to decide between the options, and that everyone comes to a satisfactory final decision. Those who 'lose' the vote have no place in the final outcome. If they are regularly in the minority, their situation is intolerable. They are under pressure to accept, or at least go along with, the majority view, against their own better judgement.

In consensus decision-making, this does not have to happen. Everyone has the opportunity – some would say responsibility – to say what they think. As each person speaks, everyone's understanding of the situation deepens. The discussion is continually redefined and reworked to assimilate each person's ideas and feelings. The options are not pre-arranged in a fixed pattern and the fluctuating process of reaching a decision includes everyone. This process is crucial and just as important as the decision. No one side 'wins', but a co-operative decision emerges, based on everyone's ideas and understanding. Deciding through consensus means that, however idiosyncratic our ideas might appear, we have a responsibility to speak them and create an atmosphere where each of us feels free to say what we really think. In this way we can all find out how we feel and what we want from a particular situation. This process opens options rather than closing them off, and leads to a greater sense of unity, which can be channelled into action. Because everyone is sure of the decision, it is possible to trust every member of the group and rely on them to provide help and support.

Where much bigger numbers are involved, briefing notes are useful as a starting point for many small group discussions. The following is a shortened version of the nonviolent direct action training notes drawn up for the blockade of the base at Greenham on 13 December 1982.

The blockade will be done by groups of women at each gate. It will be totally nonviolent. The more preparation that can be done beforehand the better the action will be. Please come prepared to be flexible and adaptable to different women's needs.

Women organising themselves into autonomous groups of about 10 makes a large decentralised action far easier to co-ordinate and service. More important, forming small groups allows women to get to know one another well; provides a basis of trust and mutual support for the action; makes decisions easier to reach; and avoids the need for 'leaders'. It also makes it easier to absorb individuals into the action at the last minute, forming the basis for a future network and future action. So please, if possible, join or form a local group.

You will be expected to provide for your own physical needs – for example, tents, warm/waterproof clothing, food, water container and transport. You will also need your own 'support' people. No matter how big or small the group, it is essential that at least three women do not do the action itself but take on the following support tasks:

● legal observer (see page 111);

● someone who will see that during action the group is fed, warm, happy – *not* exhausted, miserable and hungry – and will look after people's belongings after arrest and so on;

● someone to look after transport/communications.

Nonviolent direct actions do not have to be illegal but the blockade may be considered to be so. We may have to deal with hostility, violence and arrest. The following notes are to help your group to prepare for this. We are none of us experts and we all learn by sharing experience.

1. Exchange names, relevant experiences, fears and anxieties.

2. Make sure you understand the practical implications of action. Go through legal briefing (see pages 110–11).

3. *Before action*, think through all the other implications of what you are doing. Why are you doing this blockade? What do you hope to gain for yourself/for the movement? How will it affect other work you are doing? How do you feel about it? Sharing these feelings will help you ensure that the positives outweigh the negatives, and help sort out what roles you want to take.

4. *Action.* How will you do the action? Weave wool, link arms, sing, move, lie down? Will you talk to the police or be silent? How will you keep warm? Will you work in shifts? What do you like eating? What is it practical to eat?

How will you deal with disagreements/arguments/upsets within the group? How will you make decisions quickly?

How will you deal with confrontation? Nonviolence on your part does not, unfortunately, mean that people will treat you nonviolently. How do you feel about being kicked or shouted at? What if someone wants to talk to you? What if men want to sit down with you?

How will you support/peacekeep for each other? How will you deal with anger directed at you/coming from you?

How will you deal with arrests: going limp/total co-operation? How will you occupy yourself in a police cell?

Talking through all these questions – and there are many more – and sharing ideas and experiences will help.

Note: Pairing within a group is one form of peacekeeping. Each person can look after their partner, knowing in advance what situation they find really upsetting, and being able to support them.

A mental and emotional preparedness is not necessarily the same thing as nonviolent direct action training, which can sometimes be very mechanistic, stressing techniques, rather than talking about underlying assumptions. For some people nonviolence is just a tactic, and training sessions can, perhaps inadvertently, reinforce this idea, especially when time is short. A lot of nonviolent direct action training seems to assume that human nature is violent and aggressive, and that we must somehow overcome or subdue this. Role-playing exercises may actually set up a false situation – for example, where some people take the part of blockaders and others the police, those who play the police may be very frightened of police violence and so what they act out is a watered-down version of their own fears. This deliberately blanks out part of the real confrontation – the very humanity that nonviolence is meant to generate. What many women are stressing is that acting in a nonviolent way involves a state of mind that challenges assumptions about power. Each person has to think this through for themselves. It is the underlying attitude of mind that is important. If we have that, we will do the 'right' things at the 'right' time intuitively.

Nonviolent actions require imagination and flexibility to be able to respond as a situation develops and to keep up the pressure, not necessarily sticking to a pre-arranged plan if events render it

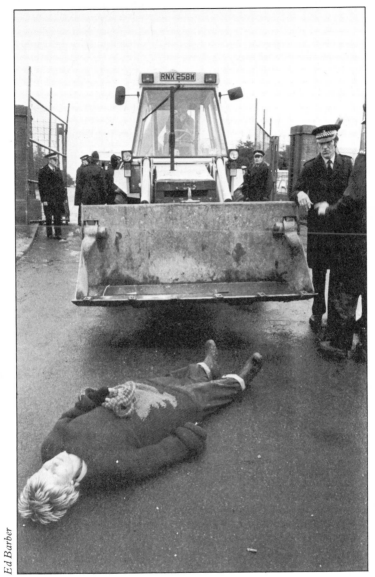

RNX 258W

Obstructing workers laying sewer pipes,
Greenham Common, 5 October 1982

ineffective. It is clearly impossible to lay down rules about this. We may decide to finish an action if there seems nothing more to gain, rather than sitting it out until we are dragged away and perhaps arrested. On occasions it may be useful for some people to get arrested to show that they are not intimidated. This will probably get further publicity and support for the action. On other occasions it may not be useful and it is certainly never necessary to be arrested to prove one's commitment. If the police are very angry we may decide not to give them any justification to use violence against us, and agree to move or leave. If they are very casual and patronising, we may want to confront them further. Sometimes it may seem appropriate to reinforce our physical presence by making a noise – humming, singing, chanting or keening. At other times silence may be more in keeping, generating a calm and dignified atmosphere. We need to be able to recognise the dynamics of a situation and decide how to behave accordingly, to achieve our purpose.

The authorities always try to impose their definition on any situation, reclaiming the initiative, and trying to define for us what we may or may not do. There is a danger that nonviolent actions such as blockades or die-ins may develop into a new orthodoxy, which becomes incorporated into what is 'acceptable' and 'allowed', as has happened with rallies and marches. Tactics, such as refusing to move when cautioned by the police or going limp on arrest, may become new 'rules' people expect to comply with, rather than choices to be made depending on the circumstances. It is necessary to focus always on what will be most effective in any particular situation. This is the challenge to our imagination and intelligence. If people really put their minds to it they can disrupt and confront without being violent.

Our obvious strength is that there are potentially so many of us, but unpredictability is equally important. The authorities simply do not expect to be continually challenged in creative, nonviolent ways. We can always take them by surprise, for they cannot anticipate what we will decide to do next. In this sense people do not know their own strength. We do not know what we can do because very few people have given it enough thought or begun to translate their ideas into action.

Nonviolence is not just the absence of violence or simply a tactic, but a total approach to living, both an ideal to aim for and a strategy for change. We cannot achieve peace through violence. It is a fundamental contradiction in terms. Means and ends merge into one another and cannot be separated, so that anything won by violence has the seeds of that violence contained within it. In any case, the state can always meet violence with far superior violence through an extensive system of law, courts, police and, ultimately, the army. If we are saying that nonviolence is a possibility, that weapons are unnecessary, that nations as well as individuals can settle differences of opinion without resorting to violence, then we undermine our own argument if we use violence, for we show that even we – who profess a commitment to nonviolence – are not capable of it ourselves.

Nonviolence involves the idea of power stemming from our only real resources – our feelings, ideas, and ultimately our bodies – drawing on imagination and determination. No one individual should have any more power than anyone else; we are all dependent on each other's knowledge and skill. By contrast, people are used to thinking that power comes from independence, from controlling knowledge, from depriving others, from other people's dependence and acquiescence. Besides physical violence there is exclusion from affection, emotional blackmail, bartering of love, which are all part of a context that recognises the right of the powerful to coerce. Nonviolence suggests that power partly derives from our relationships with each other, and recognises our fundamental mutual dependence.

Without questioning the 'success' of violence in solving problems, many people assume that nonviolence cannot be effective. Much nonviolent action is symbolic, and it is true that there has been no really widespread, systematic campaign of nonviolent direct action in this country. But it is worthwhile asking what 'effectiveness' means. Actions are clearly effective when those involved in them experience their capabilities and their strength. That exciting feeling of empowerment is something that cannot be taken away. It becomes part of how we think about ourselves, as purposeful, effective people who can express ourselves clearly on an issue of vital importance. Speaking out is a liberating experience, both for ourselves and for others who identify with what we are saying. It affirms their beliefs and encourages them to speak out too. The campaign against cruise missiles is also effective in the sense that it is continually growing. More and more people are finding ways to express their opposition to nuclear warfare. Only through nonviolent means can we create a moral and political climate where such things become unthinkable.

Clearly this is an enormous task, which involves a complete rethinking of many fundamental assumptions. Violence is so ingrained in every aspect of society that ideas about nonviolence are often scornfully dismissed as naive and utopian. Yet violence, whether in protest against nuclear weapons or conflicts between nations, ultimately solves nothing. It merely redefines and extends conflict so that it becomes more entrenched. At root it only generates more violence.

A Memo for Peace

This poem is dedicated to the women at the Greenham peace camp; and to all those who live their lives in the struggle for peace and freedom.

let us assume
that the basic assumptions
are wrong

the assumptions
    that our leaders
    and politicians
    are right
    and we
    are wrong

    that those in power
    know what's best
    for us
    that they have
    our interests
    at heart (what if
    we assume
    that they have
    no hearts?)

    that They are Good
    and Grown Up and Wise
    and we are Bad
    and Stupid Children
    needing to be
    put down
    put right
    and shown
    How To Behave

Let us assume that
that is
not so
and let us
turn those assumptions

on their heads
til they rattle and groan
and beg for mercy
and for our
forgiveness

and let us remind ourselves
that we are many

who struggle
who cry out
who suffer in silence
even those who burned
to remind us
who march on marches
picket embassies
campaign and demonstrate
sign the petitions
write to newspapers
lobby MPs

who often go unheard

who join hands
who sing the songs
who write the words
who play the music
who surround the barricades
with clowns with children
who weave coloured ribbons
between the barbed wire
who offer flowers
to the guards
who light the candles
singing softly into night

who go to jail
we
who believe
in peace
and uphold the dignity
of human life
the sanctity
of our planet

who condemn
the killings
the rapes
the missiles
the poisons
the violations
the tortures
the cover-ups
the distortions
the pornography
the lies

the basic assumptions

we need to remind ourselves
that we cannot all
be wrong

and we who live with conscience
despite the discomforts
who raise our voices
despite the silencings

who gather strength
despite the pain

we who challenge
the basic assumptions

survive

beneath
the warmongers'
icecold indifference
the politicians'
stonefaced rhetoric
the uniform armed alertness

we rattle
and keen

cry out
one voice

for peace

Viv Wynant, 20 November 1982

Why women

I want to say very strongly that having women's actions in my view has got nothing to do with excluding men. It's got to do with – for once, just once – giving women a chance, *including* women. It's so women – who have been kept out of politics and all walks of life for so long, who've been pushed back into the home and been told that they can only function in one small closed-in area to do with children and nurturing – can come out of those areas and take part in politics and actually begin to affect and change the world, and that's Why Women . . . It's positive. It's so that women can get together. Women have been isolated as individuals for so long. They've had to struggle to join together and work on issues. This way women can join together. Hundreds of women can join together and find their strength, and it's essential at this point in our history that women's strength is utilised and seen and works and is regarded as important.
Katrina Howse, March 1982

The strength of the women's community at Greenham has been particularly important during the second winter, when women lived under very difficult conditions, sleeping under plastic, living out in the rain and mud, continually harassed by the authorities. It is a remarkable manifestation of women's determination, courage and support for each other. The majority of adults in this country are women (52 per cent in 1982) but most women do not take an active part in politics, or are only peripherally involved. As time has passed it has become abundantly clear that Greenham is so successful *because* it is a women's peace camp.

It should not be at all surprising that women are involved in a campaign of nonviolent direct action, for nonviolence and feminism have some important principles in common. They both involve nonhierarchical, decentralised ways of organising, based on individual initiative, together with a recognition of our interdependence and the power of co-operation. This means that we want to work in supportive ways, sharing tasks, encouraging and caring for each other, respecting each other's ideas and experience, deciding things together. There is no role for permanent, separate leaders or experts. Since we all want the opportunity to develop and express ourselves, we should allow that opportunity to others. This may seem idealistic and in practice there are difficulties in this way of working, only too familiar to anyone who has tried it. It needs time to talk things over properly, to get to know one another, to decide things. There needs to be scope for individual initiative, without a few confident, assertive people taking over. We need to trust each other and respect our differences. While nonviolence involves caring and listening, it does not mean indulging people who are demanding, avoiding a difficult discussion or pretending things are all right when they are not. Rejecting centralised, hierarchical structures for informal ways of working can set up other kinds of exclusiveness based on strong personalities, women who are very articulate or dominating, cliques of close friends, or new rituals that become ends in themselves. Some women may feel frustrated in unstructured meetings with loose, seemingly rambling discussions. Many enjoy singing together and forming circles, and feel strengthened by it, but this does not appeal to everyone. Having said this, however, it is obvious that this way of working has great strengths and does include women in a way that other formal organisations do not.

Many women are justifiably sceptical of politicians or feel daunted and excluded by political parties, trade unions or CND groups, with their procedures, rules, committees, chairmen, written resolutions, impersonal discussions and agendas planned in

Brenda Prince

Women's Peace Camp, Greenham Common,
October 1982

advance. Most women have little experience of this way of working and often find it alienating and frustrating, as, indeed, do many men. Women respond emotionally to each other and to this crucial life-and-death issue, and do not tend to get bogged down in procedure or technical details about nuclear weapons. Obviously facts are useful, but they can sometimes become an end in themselves, a source of power and mystification, obscuring the need to try to do something about the situation.

I came to Greenham Common through the women's peace group in Sheffield. When we heard about cruise missiles, we decided to have a meeting about it. We were a fairly mixed group of women but very anxious about this issue. Our responses were almost entirely gut reactions against the whole idea of cruise missiles and all that they represented. I and one or two others had been involved in the peace movement before. Quite a lot of us hadn't been. We were feeling very angry and confused. We had a meeting and we talked. Some of the women wept in anger and frustration. This issue is very difficult for many women. They have a sudden shock of realisation. They don't have any background information. All they know is how they feel about it. They don't have any statistics; they don't have any facts.

Maybe, they think, 'I'll go along to my local CND meeting' – that's if they know one exists. They find that it's a very bureaucratic set-up, invariably run by blokes. There's a table at the top of the room and rows of seats. We all sit down and we are *informed* and we find ourselves talking to the backs of each other's heads. In that atmosphere, if you're a woman with no background to the peace movement, no political background at all, you go in and you sit at the back. You think, what I'm feeling is fear, panic, terrible distress. I want to express what I'm feeling, but there's no space for me to do it here. What are these blokes going to say? I can't stand up and cry. I can't stand up and scream. I can't even ask what I can do. They're all going on about SS-20s, missiles, rockets, the next demonstration, all kinds of political things that I don't understand. How am I going to find someone who feels the way I do? They don't seem to *feel* about it. All they seem to do is work with their heads. Some of us in our peace group have some experience of how women's groups work. Some of us didn't have that, but we were able to use what we knew – a completely different way of doing things. We *never* sat in rows. We introduced ourselves and tried to keep

the groups fairly small. If there were 25 or 30 women we would split up into smaller groups to talk. Everybody gets the chance to express themselves and their feelings. In the early days there were a lot of very distressed women, but there was space for them to express their emotions. And these things need to be done before you can sort out in your mind a plan of action for yourself.

Lesley Boulton, June 1982

By now we are involved in a widespread campaign that extends all over Britain, a decentralised network, growing all the time. Some women live at Greenham for days or months at a time. Others stay for a few days or visit occasionally, but support the camp in hundreds of ways, including raising money, publicising actions, writing to newspapers, taking photographs. Many belong to women's peace groups where they live. Besides initiating their own activities, local groups organise in their areas in preparation for large-scale actions, telling others about them, holding planning meetings and workshops, arranging childcare and transport. Equally important, small friendly groups give emotional support and encouragement.

The women's peace camp was originally set up on the basis of individual responsibility and initiative and this principle continues to be fundamental. At the same time, working together and keeping in contact with each other is vital. For local groups it is probably clear-cut who constitutes the collective, but it is less so for the peace camp itself, where women come and go. Potentially the collective could include anyone who has ever lived there. In practice, there are meetings at the camp and any woman who is interested is welcome to attend. There are also action planning meetings, often in Newbury and London, and in other towns. Particular groups tend to come together to plan an action and then send out information inviting others to take part. Ideas are discussed in smaller groups and passed on. There are no directives from above, and there is a framework provided for others to join in if they want. There is no 'official policy' beyond a shared commitment to women's actions and nonviolence.

The original march from Cardiff to Greenham Common was organised by women, calling themselves Women for Life on Earth. A few men went on the march and there were men living at the peace camp in the early months, but most of the women felt that the way they wanted to run the camp would be jeopardised if men continued to live there. As a result, since February 1982, the camp has been exclusively a women's space. This decision was much debated, both at the time and since. It has been a source of great strength to thousands of women, but also a source of misunderstanding, alienation and hurt for some women and many men. One argument is that women's action is divisive, that the issue is too important to be left to women, or that we have no right to claim a separate space. Others maintain that men are perfectly capable of behaving nonviolently, or that the world will only change when men also take responsibility for nurturing and caring and are able to develop this side of themselves. While these last two points may have some validity, some women argue that we have helped men for far too long. It is their responsibility to develop caring and sensitive ways of thinking and acting, while we as women take the lead in this fight against extinction. Many women want a space where they can express themselves, develop confidence in working together and discover new ways of organising which are personal and informal. This is evidenced by the thousands of women who are involved with the peace camp or women's actions because they are *women's* actions.

The fact is that vast numbers of women identify with Greenham, and are prepared to engage in direct political activity often for the first time, because it is a women's initiative and builds on rather than suppresses women's strength. Embracing the base on 12 December 1982 spoke directly to women – decorating the perimeter fence with symbols of life was an idea that most women found inspiring. The strength of this action was that it was possible to incorporate the diversity of 30,000 individual responses into a strong and unified statement. All of us involved with Greenham have different backgrounds, but we are all affected by being women in a man's world. Different women want to take part in women's actions for different reasons. For some it is a matter of principle, for others largely a matter of strategy.

Sir – 'War is the male prerogative apparently, the most unacceptable face of patriarchy', says L. J. O'Carroll (Letters, December 30). Sarcasm. However, I notice this is true. I notice women don't, as a social group, kill each other in wars. I notice men do. I also notice that Mr O'Carroll is frightened of women holding hands with each other instead of with him, and by the

idea of a ' "baby-care" world-view' predominating.

I don't think any of this is biologically inevitable. I don't think that all men accept the war game or that all women reject it. I do think that for thousands of years society has been dominated by men as a sex, and that this has given us a split humanity.

Almost all of recorded history so far has been a series of men-only demonstrations, in which men have taken our property rights in the earth, in women, in children, in other men.

We have to say no to the men in power and to their claim on us, and we have to say it together, in solidarity as women, because it is by splitting us off from one another that men have put us at their disposal.

This sounds exaggerated; it is only as exaggerated as these images: a mother crying alone in a room because she is suddenly intensely aware that she may not be able to protect her child from a hideous nuclear death; nappies and teddy-bears hanging on the perimeter of a nuclear base.

There was a lot of singing by the women at Greenham Common that Sunday [12 December 1982]: I know I wasn't the only woman to find my voice there. It felt like a reclamation of life. Men can do it too – but not by trying, as so many times before, either to say it for us (better), or to shut us up. Yours sincerely,
Liz Knight
The *Guardian*, 5 March 1983

The world's major power blocs led by the Soviet Union and the USA oppose each other as if they were genuine opposites, as if to distract our attention from the fact that their similarities are much more striking than their differences. Each pours vast wealth – money, natural resources and brain power – into researching, producing, stockpiling and guarding ever more diabolical means of killing people. Nightmarish weapons which are continually counted, compared, gloated over, boasted and lied about. This sick *men*tality runs through every aspect of society – British, American, Soviet. It is based on greed, arrogance, cynicism, competitiveness and irresponsibility. It reduces people to the level of things and gives machines – clocks, dictaphones, assembly lines, computers – control over us. It disciplines and stereotypes us in the name of education; manipulates

our ideas and opinions through adverts, the papers and television. When we break down we go to the doctor's to be fixed,
like cars to a garage. 'Reason' and 'science' are glorified and
slavishly followed at the expense of feeling, intuition and spiritual insight. Animals are reared to be slaughtered in barbaric
conditions. Air and water are polluted with poisonous 'wastes'.
In the name of sterile, meaningless abstractions like patriotism
and duty, mothers' sons are sent off to murder other mothers'
sons. The police, the armies and the courts are all 'only obeying
orders'. People in Africa, India and South America starve while
these same continents export shipload after shipload of tea,
coffee, meat, exotic fruit and vegetables to the rich countries of
the world. This is 'civilisation as we know it', the 'peace' they are
so proud about. We are left in isolation to deal with this system,
this outrage, with its privilege, exploitation and rape. If we can't
cope with it we're made to feel that we're weak, inadequate,
over-sensitive. The world is run by a handful of mad old men,
indulging their ghoulish, expansionist fantasies. Disenfran-
chised women, despite the vote, we are campaigning against
cruise missiles, but in doing so we are also taking on the world.
Gwyn Kirk, April 1983

For many women the issue is about reclaiming power for
ourselves, and not remaining victims of a male-defined world
characterised by violence. While women feel saddened and pessimistic about the possible consequences of this violence all around
us, it also makes us angry when we see what is going on in the
world. It is often anger that forces us out of our feelings of powerlessness, and this anger has led many women to reject any involvement with men over this issue. The focus of Greenham has mobilised thousands of women and we are spreading this energy, finding
ways to reach thousands more. It is vital that we recognise the
diversity of women involved as a source of strength. We see the
future and the role women have to play in the fight against nuclear
weapons very differently.

Some look to women's tradition as 'carers': as mothers,
teachers, looking after the elderly and the sick. They argue that
this traditional role makes it impossible to contemplate mass
destruction, perhaps even of the planet itself.

I think that most women are really in touch with what life is
about. You can't even contemplate having a child without con-

sidering the value of that life and the struggle people have bringing up children, putting in all those hours and hours of caring. A lot of women do that not even with children, but with the home, making a wonderful place for people to get by day-to-day living. You just can't contemplate that being destroyed by some people's fear and the difference in ideologies of different countries. It just doesn't make sense. Life is so much more precious than that. Also, women can identify with women of Russia and Eastern bloc countries. We're just the same. A woman in Russia is the same as myself – the same emotions, leading the same sort of life. In no way will I be part of anything that will murder her. The myth that's been put around so long that we need armies, we need these missiles, men must protect women and children from other men in other countries. That's just completely out of hand. Women must come out and say

'We don't want this type of protection. It's this type of protection which is actually endangering our lives.'

We have to find our own strength, ways of using our energy whereby we can actually change the situation because it's a very, very small minority of people making these decisions, not taking into account people's lives – playing with our lives. The majority of people in this country don't want this. What we're doing here is a consciousness-raising thing, particularly for women, because most women don't take an active part in politics. They allow their lives to be run by rules and regulations, by parliament – mainly by the male structure. What we're saying is that women are powerful. We can all come out and say 'You can't do this to us.'

Sarah Green, March 1982

Some think of this role in a more mystical sense, a belief in women's spiritual insight and connectedness to the forces of life. This strand has roots in the earliest matriarchal religion which Judaism and, later, Christianity denigrated as 'paganism'. Some see the campaign against cruise misiles as part of their wider opposition to all forms of male violence. Some believe that women have innate good qualities and are better qualified than men to take up this issue. Others feel that women are less aggressive and more caring on account of their conditioning rather than any innate biological characteristics. Finally, on a tactical level, women's actions force the authorities – the government, courts and police –

Breaching the peace, Greenham Common,
27 August 1982

Ed Barber

to deal directly with women, which they are not used to doing.

Many women believe that nonviolent direct action is more likely to stay nonviolent if only women are involved. Of course, there are some men who understand nonviolence, just as there are some women who do not, but they may be more likely to provoke violence merely by being men. Many men are afraid of violence from other men, and the police, military personnel or construction workers are more likely to use violence against men than against women.

It is a tragedy that people should waste time and energy arguing about whether or not there should be mixed actions – women and men together – at Greenham, when there is so much to be done. There are 102 other American bases in this country, and a dozen other peace camps that need support. Hundreds of firms and 1.5 million people are involved in the arms industry in Britain in one way or another. Then there are the associated dangers of nuclear power stations, the reprocessing, transporting and dumping of nuclear waste, to mention only a few things that need challenging and changing.

The different attitudes and experiences that enrich and strengthen the women's peace movement as a whole also lead to criticism from both sides: for being too feminist and for not being feminist enough. Obviously women who have spent years talking about feminism and being politically active will have a very different perspective from women who have never been directly involved in politics before. Each will come across attitudes that are hard to identify with. Many women have become involved because of their children or grandchildren. Most expect motherhood to be important for women in the future, though many hope to see the responsibility for childcare shared more. Others reject motherhood as an option and certainly as women's destiny. Still others do not want personal relationships with men. These different perspectives give rise to differences of opinion and emphasis, and to continuing, sometimes bitter, discussion. The important thing is that we build on what we share as women, our fear, commonsense, determination, and hope, developing our creativity and strength, while recognising and respecting our differences.

A public debate?

A group of women, children and men left Cardiff on 27 August 1981, to march 125 miles to USAF/RAF Greenham Common near Newbury, in protest at NATO's decision to site American cruise missiles there in December 1983. When they arrived 10 days later, they asked for a televised debate on this issue. This request was refused and so the peace camp was set up as a direct protest against cruise missiles and to get wider publicity. On 1 January 1983, people all over the world saw women dancing on a missile silo at Greenham on the television news.

In the intervening months there was some interest from local papers, local radio and television, sympathetic freelance writers and photographers, journalists and film crews from abroad, and occasional reports in the national media. Throughout the peace camp's first year, freelance writers and photographers found it virtually impossible to get mainstream newspapers or magazines to use their work. A Dutch television programme about Greenham so inspired a group of women in Holland that they decided to set up a women's peace camp at Soesterberg in May 1982, but this programme was not shown in Britain.

The national media only really began to take an interest in mid-November 1982, when 23 women were found guilty of breaching the peace for occupying the security box inside the main gate of the base in August and for obstructing work on new sewer pipes in October. By a coincidence of timing, two weeks after this there were large-scale actions at Greenham: embracing and closing the base on 12 and 13 December. Suddenly the 16-month-old protest was news and reporters scrambled over each other to catch up on some of the background. At long last a public debate had begun.

As the peace movement has grown in size and strength, government propaganda against it has had to become more blatant. In January 1983, the government talked of mounting a £1 million advertising campaign to push its 'defence' policy. Politicians from opposing parties – Labour, Liberal and SDP – as well as national CND, vociferously condemned this idea. In any case it was hardly necessary, as the goverment has access to the vast resources of the mainstream media, and already puts out its policies, especially to schools, through its Central Office for Information.

Television and radio programmes are particularly powerful. They are also very transient compared to newspapers which you can keep and look at again. You get *impressions* rather than precise information because it is difficult to remember a lot of facts and figures when they are only said once. The order in which the news items are presented is also very important in contributing to the overall impression we retain.

A very clear example of this occurred on ITN's *News at Ten* on Thursday 31 March 1983. CND organised two blockades on this day at Greenham Common and at Burghfield (also in Berkshire, where Trident warheads are being made). On Good Friday, 1 April, there was a 14-mile 'human chain' linking Burghfield, Aldermaston (the nuclear weapons research establishment which also produces nuclear warheads) and Greenham Common. The following reports were culled from newspapers, but they are presented in the order chosen by *News at Ten*:

*The expulsion of three Russians for spying – two diplomats and a journalist. Five Russians have been expelled from this country in the past four months. The Russians, two of whom were interviewed, said that the charges were ridiculous.

*The breaking of the blockade at Greenham Common airbase in Berkshire by the police.

*A report of Mrs Thatcher's reply to a question in parliament: 'It would make far more sense for these women to go and link hands

Women lay siege to Stock Exchange

The Standard Monday 7 June 1982

WOMEN demonstrators, including actress Susannah York, blockaded entrances to the Stock Exchange today in a peace protest.

Police made 10 arrests as the women, daubed with red paint, lay down in the streets around the building.

The 40 demonstrators, including several women from the long-running sit-in outside Greenham Common air base, timed their protest to mark President Reagan's visit to Britain.

Ms York said: " As a member of the peace movement, I have to try to help stop Cruise missiles, Trident, and all nuclear weapons systems.

" We want to try to take our lives back into our own hands and safeguard our children's future."

The demonstration ended peacefully after police threatened to arrest the whole group.

A spokesman for the women said: " There has been no trouble with the police and no violence. We have decided not to make any more moves today.

The Stock Exchange was chosen because its members controlled the money invested in arms industries to create nuclear weapons.

However . . .

There were nine arrests

Nobody was daubed with red paint

There were about 70 demonstrators

The Women's Peace Camp

The police didn't threaten to arrest the whole group

A spokes*man* for the women?

No-one would have said 'we have decided not to make any more moves today'

---

round the Berlin wall, if by doing so they can persuade the Soviets to take it down, to remove the guns, the dogs, and the mines there to kill people attempting to escape to freedom. If they do not succeed in this way they will prove that the freedom of the women of Greenham Comomn and of all our people needs to be defended.'

*A report of the Secretary of State for Defence Michael Heseltine's visit to Berlin. He said, 'I have a simple message for those watching the protests: raise your eyes above the demonstrators and banners and look over their heads to the Berlin wall – for this represents the real world. This is where the marching has to stop. There will be no protests behind this wall.'

As the cold war atmosphere between East and West intensifies, diplomats from different countries are being expelled on a tit-for-tat basis. What a convenient time to announce the decision to expel three more from Britain and for Heseltine to spend two days in Berlin. It seems no accident of editing that Thursday's blockades and the human chain planned for Good Friday were sandwiched between these others 'events', thus creating a context supporting the government's view that Britain needs a 'deterrent' against the 'Soviet threat'.

Most people do not have any direct contact with the press until they become involved in some kind of campaign. It is only then that you realise that getting media coverage is not a straight-forward matter. Hundreds of journalists have visited the peace camp since it started. In September 1982, the caravans were removed in a second attempt to evict the women and since then they have lived very much in the open, where everything they do is potential 'copy'. The press are specifically invited to cover particular actions. Since the autumn of 1982 a lot of this work has been co-ordinated from London as well as Greenham. Some women work hard to get media interest, preparing press releases and telephoning newspapers and magazines. Not everyone wants to talk to the press. Some people do not feel sufficiently confident. Some are exhausted with answering the same questions time and again or are sceptical about what will be published. Others want to communicate directly with those responsible for the situation – individual construction workers, politicians, police or military personnel – without going through an intermediate channel which they consider an unnecessary diversion.

Press coverage, or lack of it, plays a crucial part in any political campaign in helping to mould public opinion, though the apparent advantage of being able to reach millions of readers and viewers has to be weighed against the inherent danger of misrepresentation. It is very difficult to see the bias in reporting. It is only when you are involved in something that gets media coverage that you can compare your own experience and knowledge of it with how it is reported, and see what the discrepancies are.

The reports have been mixed and, taken together, they add up to a confusing barrage of inconsistent information. Between December 1982 and February 1983, several national papers did a peace camp 'feature', stressing the squalid conditions and the women's practical clothes.

Many articles do not go into details as to why the peace camp is there but have plenty to say about the women. The descriptions of the camp and the quotes may or may not be accurate, but they are taken out of context and reported together with anecdotes, the writer's reactions and asides.

Journalists, photographers and editors act as a highly selective filter for information, and control how people and issues are presented to a wider public. Whatever is published or broadcast has enormous authority. Reporters are not superhuman. They cannot be in two places at once or, for example, see all the way round the nine-mile perimeter fence at Greenham. Yet they talk and write as if they do see and understand everything. As outside observers they usually have little information or understanding about how an action is organised or what those involved feel about it. They never admit this limitation even if they are aware of it. They take people's experience and ideas and recreate them in another context, screening out certain points and introducing others from different contexts. We do not speak directly to the audience but through screens, which vary somewhat from editor to editor. Something of what is said gets through – more or less coherently – but muddled up with other, often louder 'voices'.

Some reporters admire the women's commitment and imagination. Others are hostile but cannot ignore the women, so aim to neutralise and suppress what they are doing, by passing them off as well-meaning but deluded, childish, muddleheaded, ignorant of life's realities, reckless and irresponsible, or simply as communists. Some make out that the women, and the Western peace movement generally, are in the pay of the USSR and interweave their report with remarks about Moscow and the Kremlin.

Others claim that they are freaks, hippy layabouts, social misfits, living on social security, or living like gypsies. This serves two purposes. It allows men (and a few women) to express their hatred of independent women in clichés:

'strident feminists', 'burly lesbians' (The *Sun*, 14 December 1982),
'hefty ladies . . . a fairly gruesome bunch' (*The Spectator*, 1 January 1983),
'the harridans of Greenham Common' (*The Spectator*, 8 January 1983),
'Amazon waifs and strays' (letter to *Newbury Weekly News*, February 1982).

All of these remarks are also designed to alienate so-called 'ordinary' women and, of course, men. The message is clear: 'You, reader,

are not like this, so you will not want to know what these women are talking about.'

The photos chosen to illustrate newspaper articles reinforce the text. This raises an important dilemma. People want to express themselves without worrying about how they might be represented, but photos of women with, for example, very short hair, dungarees, 'unusual' clothes or painted faces, which some women like and which anyway are thought of as a personal matter, are used by unsympathetic editors as part of this stereotyping and undermining process.

News reporting of the arrests and trial of the 44 women who climbed on to the missile silo on New Year's Day devoted a lot of space to the 'emotional scenes' inside and outside the court – the dancing, singing, hugging, and crying. Emotional response is presented as something to gawp at, typically female, weak and irrational. Of course women were angry and upset as the magistrates and police got on with just-doing-their-job. Of course we want to encourage each other to confront the military insanity going on all around us and upheld by these same magistrates and police. Those present describe how the authority of the court was completely overturned for them by the atmosphere of joyful defiance, despite the inevitability of the sentences.

Only The *Guardian* (3 January 1983) reported that the women risked charges under the Official Secrets Act. Only The *Morning Star* (16 February 1983) reminded readers that each cruise missile is 15 times as lethal as the bomb dropped on Hiroshima in 1945.

A second example of highly selective reporting occurred in accounts on 14 December 1982 of the mass blockade at Greenham on the previous day. The women's complete nonviolence was ignored entirely. Police violence was mentioned but with the suggestion that this was somehow forced on them by the women, rather than a deliberate choice. The police

'tried to cool the situation' (*Daily Express*),
'tried to preserve a delicate balance' (The *Guardian*),
were 'caught in the crush' (*Daily Mirror*),
were 'struggling' while they 'tried desperately to maintain a good humoured presence',
they 'decided to avert a situation whereby hundreds of women might end up behind bars' (*Daily Telegraph*).

The press has a fixation about arrests. The *Daily Telegraph* even headlined its account of this blockade: 'Peace women fail to get arrested.' This emphasis is a gross and dangerous distortion because it glamourises dramatic actions and judges them by irrelevant standards. It completely overlooks whether those involved in an action feel it has succeeded in making its point, or even what that point is. It may also make some women feel that they have to get arrested to demonstrate their commitment. Many do not want to, and they are not weak or useless because of it.

Another kind of distortion is the habitual reference to leaders. Journalists like leaders and where there are no obvious leaders they create them – even to the extent of referring to 'a spokes*man* for the women . . .'! It is obviously much more convenient to deal with one or two people, especially if you can get them on the end of the telephone when you want them. Loose, non-hierarchical ways of organising are unfamiliar and it takes time and effort to talk to a range of people, sometimes genuinely impractical with tight deadlines. As one reporter exclaimed in frustration about the organisation of the actions on 12 and 13 December 1982: it's all so 'damned decentralised'. Reporters want concise, 'authoritative' statements,

Claire Hershman

Nonviolent blockade of the base, Greenham Common,
13 December 1982

preferably with a minimum of trouble. Leaders are assumed to speak with authority and talking to them contributes to the reporter's 'omniscience'.

While all this is particularly true of the national media, it is not always the case in the local press and magazines with smaller circulations and a different political perspective. For many people, the local newspaper is the chief source of news. There is not the same pressure on space in local papers and it is generally much easier to get journalists to cover local groups and actions. Letters pages are one of the most popular items in local papers, and many women have used this as an opportunity to get their ideas across. This article from the *Chester Chronicle* is a good example of women using local media resources to publicise their group and advertise their ideas.

Peace has to be something today's women care about, whatever form the concern takes . . . in Chester there is now an effective Women for Peace Group which offers a channel for both concern and action . . .

Denise Aaron, mother of three young children, brought together 13 like-minded women in the sitting room of her home for a meeting in September 1981, and thus the Chester Women for Peace Group was born.

It has prospered. At the last count 300 newsletters went out and on 12 December, three coachloads went to join the day of protest at Greenham Common. And there are plans for a mammoth women's march from Chester to Greenham Common to arrive at the base for Hiroshima Day on 6 August.

Group meetings are now getting so large that there is a plan for splinter neighbourhood units, but everyone will still get together regularly for planning purposes – and the pleasure of seeing so many united in a cause.

There are no leaders, everything being done through co-operation. At meetings members always sit in a circle and one person (different each time) acts as 'facilitator', drawing up the agenda, making sure all runs smoothly, checking everyone who wants to have a say, and, in particular, drawing in newcomers.

The group is broad based . . . Members believe that, as women alone, they can achieve more, and securing their children's future is a common driving force.

Denise says that, being all women, they get emotional support from each other.

'We come along in the first place because we are worried sick about the nuclear arms race, and one of the first things we need is understanding, comfort and support from others who feel the same.'

'This is what gives us the solidarity to go out and face people who are hostile to us, on the streets or at meetings or knocking on people's doors. It can be lonely out there.'

Members of the Chester group tend to do their own thing, ranging from leafletting houses to organising street theatre sessions on a peace theme. They fund-raise to finance their own efforts, and write letters all the time, to newspapers, MPs, councillors, civil defence planners, the prime minister, even, recently, Prince Charles.

They go out on the streets to talk to people and find that in the 15 months since the group was formed, there has been a switch in people's attitudes. People are much better informed, and they are concerned and ready to listen . . .

There are many local magazines that report women's actions in a more sympathetic manner than the national press, and anti-nuclear magazines like *Peace News* and *Sanity* give a lot of space to the women's peace network. Feminist publications like *Spare Rib* and *Outwrite* have carried many reports on Greenham and feminist views on nonviolence. The *New Statesman* has published various articles over the last few months on women's actions and the legal system and the peace camp.

Whatever the publication, all events at a particular time compete with each other for 'newsworthiness'. Even some 'hardened' press people found the embrace of the base on 12 December interesting and moving, but they were not interested when women handed out peace pies outside the Bank of England at lunchtime on 8 March, International Women's Day, though this generated constructive conversations about peace with passers-by. Nor did the press want to know about women from Greenham who had been brutally treated by the police at Comiso in Sicily, another site in Europe which is expected to receive cruise missiles in 1983. As these examples show, actions deemed to be of sufficient public interest must fulfil certain criteria. Of course this does not mean that actions which do not get reported at all are less valuable – the criteria certainly bear no relation to the strength and significance of action.

As well as journalists' accounts, there have been hundreds if not thousands of letters sent to editors of newspapers all over the country, giving information; putting personal points of view, both supportive and critical; discussing women's actions or the importance of nonviolence – all contributing to a continuing public debate, and often correcting or challenging earlier news reports or editorials.

Male domination

Daily Telegraph 13 December 1982

Many brought husbands and menfriends with them unaware that this was also intended to be a day of protest against the male dominated society.

The message was made clear to any men who dared to approach the demonstrators gathered around the main gate of the base.

" No men allowed here " barked a tough looking guard who was barely recognisable as being of the appropriate gender herself.

Men were more wel...
East Gate wh...

Daily Express 13 December 1982

'A Russian TV crew filmed the mass anti-nuclear protest by women at Greenham Common yesterday . . .

As the Soviet cameras rolled, the 30,000 demonstrators milling in the mud appeared as unwitting dupes of a propaganda coup by Moscow . . .

Later the Moscow TV crew were huddled in earnest conversation with some of the organisers of the demo . . .

Daily Star 14 December 1982

THE women of peace found themselves at war yesterday.

They battled with hundreds of police outside the Greenham Common air base.

Several people were hurt during the scuffles and three demonstrators were arrested. But last night the b...
women were claim...

Sunday Telegraph 12 December 1982

...an missil...
...cause they are pre—
...u — in practice if not in theory — to put peace at risk. Peace-mongering and warmongering are the two faces of the same false coin, both of which are equally mindless and menacing, not to say obscene. Hell hath no fury like a peacewoman scorned, by comparison with whom even a Cruise missile becomes a soft symbol of sweetness and light.

I went to Greenham Common. As an individual I decided it was time I voiced my protest, expressed my opinion in a way that would be heard. This seemed to be the view expressed by all the women on our bus (and the two gentlemen who came along to look after the children). We shared a feeling of purpose, of hope, along with our fears of what cruise means to our children's future.

We asked which group people belonged to, and the overwhelming impression was that it was not a group they represented but themselves. There were Quakers, CND supporters, Roman Catholics, feminists, members of the Ecology Party, members of the Labour Party, Conservative women, actresses, students, grand-

101

mothers protesting for their grandchildren, and we two, Methodist women, holding hands round the camp.

This was not an 'organised' event; we were not exhorted to go, we only heard about it a week ago and it took some detective work to find out if there was anyone else going. We two were determined to go, even if it meant going on our own, each as an individual; this was the view expressed time and again, 'We would have come on our own if it was necessary.'

As it happened two coaches were booked from Barnstaple, women travelling in from villages all over the area. On the day we found that there were other coaches from Torrington, Bideford, Appledore, Holsworthy – all from an area traditionally slow to react.

We were all at Greenham Common from a personal belief, not because we had been pressurised into going, not necessarily because we are politically motivated, but because we believe that cruise missiles are an unholy and horrific weapon for anyone to contemplate using.

Margaret Bailey and Gill Weeks
Methodist Recorder, 23 December 1982

Your recent editorial and your answer to Patricia Pulham's letter both raise the tired old myth that the Peace Movement, in this case the Greenham women, are pro-Russian.

This is, if you'll excuse the phrase, a red herring. We are people (American, English, Chinese, yes, and Russian) and against nuclear weapons, whoever they belong to.

The reason why we seek to change the policy of our own country, rather than someone else's, is surely fairly obvious. We live in a democracy and are therefore responsible for our Government's actions.

In this case, our Government is forcing American-controlled missiles upon us and giving its support to American defence policy, so we have the right and, more than that, the responsibility as members of a free society to object to actions, which we deplore, being taken in our name.

The Russians have never claimed to be acting in our interests or by our mandate. Of course, we deplore Russian missiles and we are in no position to guarantee that they would not use them if we disarmed unilaterally, any more than the Government can prove that its policy does not make nuclear war more likely. We are necessarily dealing with conjecture.

One thing we can say, however. Our way is morally justifiable, the Government's is not. Blowing up or threatening to blow up innocent people is wrong, and I, for one, will not let anyone do such a thing in my name without protest.

Stephanie Bowgett
Chester Chronicle, 14 January 1983

BBC TV News carried an item (December 18) showing the good citizens of Newbury clearing up the 'rubbish' left at Greenham Common. This 'rubbish' comprised the symbols of love, hope, peace and life which I and 30,000 other women had attached to the wire fence around the base in opposition to the camp's message of hatred, despair, war, and death.

Among the items torn down was a photograph of my four daughters. It is because there are many who consider my children to be just so much rubbish that I shall continue to work for the abolition of the values and symbols of this war-crazed world.

Yours faithfully, Christine Garnier

The *Guardian*, 23 December 1982

If you decide you want to get an action publicised it is worthwhile spending some time thinking out the best ways of doing this and the pitfalls. It is often useful to write a press statement explaining the action, and for one or two women to take responsibility for making sure it is circulated and for talking to the press. The following notes from a workshop discussion may provide some useful starting points for discussions.

The vast majority of press reporters are just doing a job - getting a story. We can't rely on them to have any interest in supporting what we're doing or understanding things from our point of view. In fact it's quite often the reverse and they try to exploit what they see to be our weaknesses.

While we may want media coverage we don't just want to be passively on the receiving end of journalists' questions and comments, or simply objects of interest for photographers.

Being interviewed can be very isolating. You are singled out and under pressure to answer questions which may be irrelevant, undermining or patronising, or which misrepresent how you or others feel.

Some journalists adopt an aggressive style because they seem to think it goads people into saying what they really believe.

Usually when you're asked a question you feel some obligation to reply. It's very easy to get drawn into this, often without realising it, and to waste time talking about things you don't think are really important. Just because they ask a question you don't have to answer it if you don't want to. You can ignore it and just say what you wanted to say anyway, or turn the question round:'Oh, people don't really want to know ... what's important is when the government is going to see sense...' You can give a joke answer if you think it's a silly question, but you can't trust reporters not to print it or broadcast it.

TV reporters may be friendly and supportive to get your confidence until the cameraman is ready, and then switch completely and ask difficult or hostile questions. For example, you're outside your town hall, protesting about the council's plan for so-called 'civil defence' and suddenly you're asked: 'Surely you don't think you're doing anything constructive by sitting here today. After all the council knows what it's doing/ You're just making people angry/wasting their time/making work for the police ...' People are used to seeing TV announcers and newsreaders who speak authoritatively from a prepared script. If you fumble for words, viewers may think that you don't really know why you're there. No one will know that you just weren't expecting the question.

Press photographers - almost always men - tend to give orders: 'move over there, love', 'turn round', 'look that way'. There's always a reason why they want you to do this and it's worth looking to see what or who you'll be standing next to if you do move over there. You don't have to move.

You can sometimes refuse to be photographed, but if you're involved in an action there often isn't a choice. However, you may be able to walk away/ turn your back on the camera/walk straight up to the camera so that you're too close and the photographer will only get a close-up of your coat buttons or your nose.

Journalists and photographers may callously exploit someone's vulnerability, for example, by picking on someone who is crying. You can distract their attention/send them on a wild goose chase/mess up the shot by getting in the way - walking between the camera and the shot.

Make it clear to journalists what you think of how their paper is reporting the issue.

We cannot rely on the established media to report systematically or accurately what we are doing, and so our own communication networks are absolutely vital:

- talking to people, writing personal letters
- producing leaflets, information sheets, newsletters and magazines
- putting up posters, leaving messages in library books or

104

doctors' waiting rooms, writing on walls
- organising meetings, discussion groups, film shows and gigs
- setting up peace groups committed to nonviolent direct action
- having telephone networks for passing information
- recording events and experiences with photos, sound recordings, film and video
- making songs, poems, plays.

These are all active processes: we pass on our ideas, sharing information and experience, encouraging and affirming each other, rather than being passive consumers of official 'truth'.

This is the thinking behind the chain letter for organising the actions of 12 and 13 December 1982. Women at the peace camp sent out letters to about 1,000 women. Each woman was asked to copy the letter and send it to 10 friends who would also copy it and sent it to 10 more, so everyone was part of the organising.

This was an inspiration for many women, giving them a chance to participate on their own terms. Responsibility was not in the hands of a central organising body, but focused on each woman responding to the invitation. In this way each woman took responsibility for publicising the event and making it a success. Women heard about the actions over a period of three months; they talked about it, made phone calls, wrote letters. The information was transmitted in a lateral way, changing as it moved from one to another, remaining a living communication. This process is diametrically opposed to more standard means of communication, where a static body of information is transmitted downwards. It is an attempt to reach the vast numbers of women untouched by other networks, partly by speaking in a different language and partly by using different channels. It seemed at the time as if we were plumbing older networks of talk and rumour, and rediscovering how efficient a means of communication they are. If the information strikes a chord, it is transmitted.

The success of the chain letter at informing many thousands of women about the actions was partly to do with the information being a starting point because duplicating it, thinking whom to send it to, phoning friends, are all active processes, they open the information and enable each individual to make a real contribution, which is likely to spread to assuming greater responsibility.

In October, I received a chain letter from Greenham Common women's peace camp. I had been to the camp several times but had not taken an active part for a few months. The letter came out of the blue. It told me about the action planned for 12 and 13 December, embracing and then closing the base. The women asked me to copy the letter and send it to 10 friends, the idea being that if every woman who received one did this, then the 10,000 women needed to encircle the base would arrive on 12 December. I didn't read so-called 'impartial' information in a newspaper. This was a personal communication addressed to me, requesting things of me, making it plain that *every* woman was included, was important. Not only did I copy the letter, but I spent a long time considering who to send it to. I didn't send it to women who I thought would hear about the action anyway, nor to women who would never go to such a demonstration. I sent letters to women I thought would be interested but had not become directly involved. I felt that the spur of a personal letter might spark off enthusiasm. As it turned out, several of these women were at Greenham on 12 December. Some had not been to a demonstration before. I am sure that everyone who received the letter must have gone through the same process, ensuring that women we knew heard about the action.

I was also asked to bring something to put on the perimeter fence: 'anything related to "real" life – as opposed to the unreal world that the military base represents'. When I first read this it did not strike me as important. As the time grew closer, I increasingly found myself wondering what to take. In the end I took a photograph of my mother and some poems. Sticking them on the fence was, to my surprise, the most moving experience of the weekend. I kept seeing my mother's face on the wire fence. I often think of every single one of the 30,000 women doing the same: carefully thinking what symbol they would leave at the base.
Alice Cook, April 1983

Despite its serious limitations, media coverage has been crucial in alerting people in this country to the danger of nuclear weapons, and by December 1982 a majority were actually against cruise missiles. This has been described as 'the Greenham factor', a media phrase which manages to both acknowledge and trivialise the influence of the peace camp. Ironically, if there *had* been a tele-

How we Spin and thread ourselves together as Women for this day — To make
it strong + effective·············

You are a spring and if you copy both sides
of this letter and send them to 10 other women,
who then do the same, who then do the same, etc.
we will become rivers that will flow together on Dec.12th
and become an ocean of women's energy. Believe it
will work and it WILL work.

vised debate in September 1981 the peace camp might never have
existed and far fewer people would have known anything about
cruise missiles.

Over the months, women's actions have broken through a
barrier of media silence, but press interest can be pressurising and
seductive. It is important to continue to do things that capture
people's imagination and do not play into the hands of press slurs
or pressure to be arrested or imprisoned.

There are more than a dozen peace camps in Britain at
present, outside military bases and weapons factories, but the
media focus in on Greenham almost exclusively, at the expense of
the others – another important aspect of editorial selection.

Greenham has not been singled out for particularly bad
coverage by the media. All kinds of issues are trivialised, subjected
to the cynicism and opportunism of journalists, and editorial control. But this issue is not simply good 'copy' for a few months of
media treatment. It affects journalists personally just the same as
everyone else.

Using the law

I do not feel I stand here today as a criminal.

I feel this court is dealing in trivia by making this charge against us, while those who are the real criminals (those who deal in our deaths) continue their conspiracy against humankind. We will continue to make a peaceful stand against them and continue to uphold our moral values which celebrate life.

We are all individuals whose responsibility it is to maintain and nurture life, something all of us can do together – with mutual support.

While we stand here the silos, which are intended to house the cruise missiles from December 1983, are still being constructed at Greenham Common. We all feel the urgency of this threat to our lives – and are determined not to remain silent.

As women we have been actively encouraged to be complacent, by sitting at home and revering men as our protectors: we now reject this role.

The law is concerned with the preservation of property. We are concerned with the preservation of all

life. How dare the government presume the right to kill others in our names?

Women's statement to Newbury Magistrates Court, 14 April 1982

The decision to site US cruise missiles at Greenham by December 1983 was taken by top NATO commanders in December 1979. There was no discussion in parliament, though a few British politicians knew about the decision and supported it. Our system of government is supposed to be open and democratic. There are 'proper channels' for making our views known: voting every four or five years, writing to MPs who are supposed to represent us, forming pressure groups to campaign over particular issues. Once government policy is decided – especially, as in the case of cruise missiles, way above the heads of most MPs – the 'proper channels' are virtually useless.

This has led the women involved in the peace movement into direct action and into possible conflict with some aspect of the law. In many people's minds, there is an important dividing line between legal means of influencing government and actions that break the law. However, whether a particular direct action is deemed illegal is in the hands of the authorities. There are laws to cover virtually any situation: for example, simply standing still on the pavement can be deemed an offence.

The authorities have tried to deal with the women at Greenham Common by attempting to evict them and, sometimes, by arresting women involved in various actions and charging them with relatively minor offences – obstructing the highway, obstructing a police officer, behaviour likely to cause a breach of the peace. In reserve are more intimidating charges which carry heavier fines or prison sentences, such as offences under the Official Secrets Act which could apply to actions on or around military bases. The authorities rely on precise, often very trivial, legal technicalities. What is really on trial, however, is our freedom of speech and freedom to express political opinion, a central principle of democratic government and, ironically, exactly what the government claims to be defending with nuclear weapons.

Many people know almost nothing about the law and the courts and this lack of knowledge may be one of the most intimidating aspects of direct action to begin with. In preparing for an action, whether or not we will be breaking the law is an important consideration – what we can be arrested for and what the maximum penalties are. Women lawyers give legal advice which is usually included in a legal briefing for each action. This allows women to discuss the legal position beforehand and decide what part they want to play in the action. The following is an amended version of the legal briefing drawn up for the actions at Greenham on 12 and 13 December.

Offences for which you may be arrested

a) obstructing the highway; b) obstructing a police officer in the course of his duty; c) various public order charges, for example, breach of the peace; d) criminal damage; e) Official Secrets Act.

The first four are the offences most often used by police in enforcing order. They all carry the power of arrest and allow police to remove you from the action and possibly hold you in custody overnight. They must be heard in a magistrates' court.

In all cases we list the *maximum* penalties, but usually the penalty is a small fine or an order to be bound over to keep the peace. If you refuse to pay a fine or be bound over, you will be jailed.

a) *Obstructing the highway:* highway means any highway available to the general public, which need only be partially obstructed or obstructed by someone else because of your action. Max. penalty: £50 fine.

b) *Obstructing an officer:* useful to police when they cannot get you for anything else and almost impossible to argue with (arguing could itself constitute an offence). Max. penalty: £200 fine and/or one month in prison.

c) *Breach of the peace:* it is an offence to use 'threatening, abusive or insulting words or behaviour' either deliberately or which could cause a breach of the peace in any public place. You can be charged with this if it seems likely that a breach of the peace *might* happen. Max. penalty: 6 months in prison and/or £1,000 fine. Or the magistrate can be asked to *bind you over to keep the peace*. This will be for a specific time with the surety of a fixed sum.

d) *Criminal damage:* it is an offence to 'without lawful excuse deliberately destroy or damage property belonging to another'. Max. penalty if damage less than £200: 6 months and/or £1,000 fine. If more than £200 can be tried in crown court with max. penalty of 10 years, and/or large fine.

e) *Official Secrets Act:* this is mentioned simply to acquaint you with the remote possibility of it being used at some point in the next year against a few individuals to deter us from increasing activity. It covers 'prohibited places' which include military establishments, and UK Atomic Energy Authority establishments. There are several sections, carrying different maximum sentences ranging from 14 years to life imprisonment.

By-laws
Infringement of by-laws can only be prosecuted in the magistrates' court and normally carries a maximum fine of £50. *There is no power of arrest.*

Getting arrested
Each group should have a *legal observer* with the names and phone numbers of members of the group. This woman should observe everything that happens, keep notes and be a witness in court; *stay* with her group and *not* get arrested; note numbers of arresting officers; get in touch with a solicitor; if arrested, hand over task to someone else.

If you are arrested you are usually warned first and given the chance to leave. If you decide to stay, call your name to the legal observer. You will be taken to a police station; asked your name, address and phone number, birth date and occupation; then searched. You may be questioned but you do not have to say anything. You do not have to have fingerprints or photographs taken. Once you are charged you will probably be released. If not, don't panic – a solicitor will have been contacted by your legal observer.

Efforts by Newbury District Council to evict the women's peace camp aimed to avoid the political dimensions of the campaign by concentrating on simple squatting charges. The Council's first attempt to get a possession order to reclaim the land was heard in the High Court in London in May 1982, when the judge ruled that the issue was not a political one, that the women had no right to camp on common land, and granted the possession order. However, it was clear that the Council's hope of quietly removing the peace camp from the public eye had come too late and in fact it backfired – support was growing fast. A demonstration outside the court, and the dozens of women who added their names to the list of defendants and filled the courtroom to overflowing all testified to this. Each one of the defendants who stood up to make a statement stressed that the issue was not camping but cruise missiles. Squatting cases are usually heard in closed court. The judge relied on this practice and refused access to the press so that none of these statements could be reported.

This move was made eight months after the peace camp was established. Presumably the Council had hoped that the peace camp would fold up by itself through the previous, bitterly cold winter. A strip of land alongside the main road near the airbase is

Ed Barber

After the second eviction, Newbury District
Council tipped tons of rubble on the site of
the peace camp, September 1982

not owned by the Council but by the Department of Transport. The Council removed some caravans and destroyed a large shelter, but the women neatly circumvented the effect of the possession order by moving the camp a few yards on to the Department of Transport land. Whereas various national newspapers carried reports of this court case and photographs of protesters outside the court being dragged away by police, the continuation of the peace camp went unreported. The same thing happened in September 1982 when the camp was evicted again, this time by the Department of Transport itself. Television reports showed caravans being towed away and the camp dismantled, but there was no coverage over the next few weeks to show that women were continuing to live in the open at Greenham, back on land belonging to the Council.

This time, however, the Council decided to enforce its by-laws much more strictly. Accordingly, women were not allowed to put up any 'structures' and had to live under plastic coverings, sleeping in vans or in small benders made from branches covered with plastic, and hidden in the woods. In effect, they have been forced by the Council to live in extremely primitive conditions.

Although still arguing over by-laws, Newbury Council's next move was more hard-hitting. They first revoked the deed allowing public access to the common land. The Council then applied for a second possession order, as well as injunctions against 21 named women, forbidding them to set foot on the common land for an unlimited period or to 'conspire with others' or incite others to go there. Again, by the time the possession order hearing came to court, several hundred women had added their names to the list of defendants, and while both the possession order and the injunctions were granted (though the incitement part was dropped), the groundswell of support and counter publicity meant that the attempt to dispose of the camp backfired once again. Indeed, women just moved their things back on to the strip of land belonging to the Department of Transport, as before.

The Council decided to revoke the deed allowing public access in order to ban the 21 women from the common, thus putting themselves in the ridiculous position of making it out of bounds to anyone at all, except the few people who live around the common and have long-standing commoners' rights. Many people were angry about ths tactic.

Sir – Mr Bryan Philpott [Newbury Councillor] said (The *Guardian*, Friday 25): 'We realise we have technically taken away the right of everyone to use the common, but I am sure most of the people would regard that as a small price to pay to get rid of the camp.'

What price democracy?

We who live in Newbury find ourselves the current focus of Europe on a crucial issue for mankind. Surely it is the very freedom which Mr Philpott is sacrificing which is the bone of contention between East and West?

Are we to set about crushing opponents' rights to express themselves by mass prohibition?

Mr Philpott makes a sweeping assumption of support for this move without having the courage to expose it to debate beforehand.

It has been said that when women are allowed to join hands round the Kremlin, the West will take the peace movement seriously. Women are no longer allowed to join hands around Greenham Common. Is this a step forward?

Yours sincerely, David Hawkey

The *Guardian*, 1 March 1983

On 12 May 1983, Newbury District Council evicted the part of the peace camp that was still on their land and impounded several cars, allegedly to defray their costs. When the women lay down in the road to try to stop them moving the vehicles away, they were forcibly removed by High Court bailiffs. Despite growing harassment from the authorities, the women at the peace camp have said time and time again that they do not intend to leave. Moreover, the 21 women affected by the High Court injunction have refused to let this ruling limit them over-much. It is undoubtedly a restriction on their freedom, but unlikely to affect the peace camp. Many of these women are now very active in other ways – talking to public meetings, CND groups, working through trade unions – and there are many others organising future actions. Newbury District Council is in the process of drafting new by-laws for Greenham Common. Amongst other things, they want to fence off sections of common land, presumably as another possible line of attack against the peace camp, and to 'regulate' assemblies.

Whatever one may think of the cause embraced by the women of the Greenham Common peace camp, it is plain that the authorities have made a fearful hash of dealing with them.

The women's cause thrives on publicity and attention. The actions of the authorities, particularly those of the Newbury District Council but also those of the Ministry of Defence and the police, have ensured that the camp has got great and growing exposure.

> They are like firemen trying to put out a fire by throwing petrol on it.
> The *Observer*, 13 March 1983

Just as the Council has tried to ignore the political implications of the peace camp, so the authorities, by not pressing charges or by charging women with relatively minor offences, are trying to deny that there is any threat from the women's actions. This tactic is a way of trying to incorporate and neutralise their effect, and it may well change again over the next few months. In the early 1960s, the leaders of the 'Committee of 100' were given prison sentences of up to 18 months under the Official Secrets Act when their campaign of direct action began to expand. This seems to be the thinking behind Newbury Council's decision to get injunctions against 21 women whom they presume to be ringleaders. But the experience of the past 18 months has shown that, whatever has happened to some individual women, there have always been many more ready to commit themselves.

Those arrested at the first blockade in March 1982 were charged with obstructing the highway, and faced small fines. Some women decided to pay the fine. Others refused and were given prison sentences of a week, in practice reduced to four or five days with remission for 'good behaviour'. All through the summer individual women served these sentences with very little publicity. It was left to local police to chase them up for non-payment, and so they were dealt with separately and sent to different prisons at different times. Apart from one woman's 'sponsored' prison sentence, little appeared in the press.

This altered in November 1982 with the case of 19 women arrested for going on to the base at Greenham and occupying the security box on 27 August. They had been charged with behaviour likely to cause a breach of the peace. By an accident of timetabling, which the authorities must have regretted later, the case of 12 women arrested on 5 October for attempting to stop construction work at Greenham was also heard the same week. This meant that on three consecutive days women were given prison sentences for refusing to agree to be bound over to keep the peace.

At the first of these cases various witnesses – including E. P. Thompson and the Bishop of Salisbury – testified that the women were engaged in keeping rather than breaching the peace. Whereas they were charged under legislation dating back to 1361, the women used the Genocide Act 1969 in their defence, arguing that it is the actions of the government that are illegal, in that they are planning for genocide by agreeing to have cruise missiles in this country.

Article II of Genocide Convention
In the present Convention, genocide means any of the following acts committed with intent to destroy, in whole or in part, a national, ethnical, racial or religious group, as such:
(a) Killing members of the group;
(b) Causing serious bodily or mental harm to members of the group;
(c) Deliberately inflicting on the group conditions of life calculated to bring about its physical destruction in whole or in part;
(d) Imposing measures intended to prevent births within the group;
(e) Forcibly transferring children of the group to another group.

Women argue that they are justified in taking actions which may be seen as illegal, to counter the far greater illegality of nuclear weapons. The Genocide Act is an interesting piece of legislation – a virtually unenforceable law. While it complies with the international Genocide Convention, only the Attorney General can prosecute under it. As a member of the government, he is hardly likely to bring a case under this Act against other members of the government.

Being involved in a court case creates a lot of work, marshalling the various arguments and evidence, and preparing statements. Supportive and committed women lawyers have added immeasurably to women's confidence about all this. Women who have never before been involved with the law have found themselves dealing with the police and the courts: planning their defence, often defending themselves, making personal statements, questioning witnesses. This is possible because women are supporting each other and working together in a legal system designed to isolate people and induce feelings of guilt.

There is always a risk in hiring lawyers that everyone gets bogged down in obscure legal points. Lawyers are trained to win cases, by fair means or foul, rather than to assist their clients to say what they think is important. Women don't say what they want in that atmosphere, or it is lost in a conspiracy of professional courtroom workers.

However, the Greenham women's cases followed almost none of the patterns of the usual magistrates' court case. The first big court case was the trial on 15 November of the women who invaded the base at Greenham on 27 August. There were three lawyers (me, Liz and Izzie) involved in preparing the case

with women who had been arrested for breach of the peace. When we met the women, we were almost washed away by the huge flood of information, ideas and argument that they wanted to put over in court. Whatever the police wanted to talk about in court, it was plainly our job to put the focus of the hearing on to the issue of cruise missiles, disarmament and protest. None of the Greenham women seemed to have illusions about the courts – they don't offer justice – or about lawyers, who can't work miracles. What we were asked to do was create a framework which would enable women and their witnesses to testify as to their own knowledge and experience of the nuclear issue.

In the end, listening to the women from Greenham talking, it was plain that the emphasis of the case would have to be on the defence. So often a court case revolves around denying what the prosecution say. In a series of meetings we agreed that we were not really interested in what the prosecution would say. We would concentrate on putting forward the real reasons that led women to leave their jobs, homes, families and cross the physical and psychological barriers that keep people out of USAF bases in this country. To do this we designed a series of legal arguments about the right and duty of all of us to prevent our own government and the US government from breaking the terms of the Genocide Act 1969 (an Act of Parliament that hardly anyone had heard about before).

I had done cases with many other demonstrators before, but never anything quite like this. It wasn't that the Greenham women didn't care if they were convicted, because they did worry a lot. It was more that the issue of cruise missiles was so important that it overrode every other concern. It was something that so desperately had to be said and heard that nothing else seemed at all important. We found we were working on issues far wider than a lawyer would usually consider, instead of having to chop everything up into little bits to fit in with the court's preconceptions.

I think courtrooms are frightening places at the best of times. My experience of that is particularly as a woman working in the male-dominated legal profession. Women are treated badly by the courts – not openly, but in all the male assumptions about how business in court should be conducted. It is so easy and comfortable for men to assume and exercise power and superiority over women, and given that courts are all to do with the legitimate exercise of power, women tend to come off very badly. There are elaborate codes of behaviour in court that women are not at home in. There are special ways of being polite (courtesy) and of being rude (sarcasm and bullying) that are almost uniquely male. No one smiles very much. For women to join in, it usually means joining on men's terms. I find it very alien, and I suspect that most women lawyers really feel that too.

The triumph was that Greenham women cut through all that. They gave all the wrong responses. They laughed, cheered and clapped. They didn't take half of it seriously. I know most of the women were scared before they spoke, but in the end some things had to be said, which overcame the fear. That applied to the lawyers too, because we were very scared before the first hearing. We didn't know whether the court would let us use the Genocide Act arguments or call the witnesses who were coming along. We had no idea if we'd be thrown out of court within an hour or so of starting.

What did happen, once we'd got started in November, February and at other trials since, has changed all my feelings about courts. We took control of that environment away from the men, however briefly. It didn't mean that arguments were just put in expressive, emotional, feeling ways, though that was unusual enough. It was also seeing women make the court listen to arguments that were articulate, intellectually coherent and historically wise. Women did it by poems, by singing, and some cried while they spoke. Even policewomen were moved to tears. Everywhere there were flowers. Courtrooms hardly frighten me at all now.

But then the whole focus of my fears in life has shifted. Why should courtrooms worry anyone while the threat of utter destruction hangs over us? I sat through the 15 February case in Newbury when women scientists backed up our own knowledge with the terrifying implications of their research. I couldn't believe, then, that the magistrates would not simply step down from their table and join us. I have moved from merely being 'against the bomb' but not believing it could be changed, to joining Greenham women in stopping it.
Jane Hickman, May 1983

In the second of these cases in November, women were also charged with behaviour likely to cause a breach of the peace by obstructing construction workers attempting to lay sewer pipes outside the main gate of the base on 5 October by lying in the trenches, weaving woollen webs across them, and lying down in front of bulldozers. Several women presenting their own defence questioned construction workers, who finally admitted that the women's behaviour would not have led to any violence. Others asked, 'Who is really breaching the peace?' All these women, several of whom appeared in both cases, were found guilty and given the choice of being bound over to keep the peace for one year or going to prison for 14 days. As they refused to give assurances of 'good' behaviour, 23 of them were sent to prison. While they were split into smaller groups and sent to different prisons, they were not isolated as women had been in the summer.

This is not to say that those who have served prison sentences did not find it alienating and frightening. Many women have been badly treated in prison and in police cells and would think hard before putting themselves in that position again. All have gained strength as a result, however, and pass this on to others. What is intended as a humiliating and punishing system has become an experience from which women learn and gain power, both for themselves and for others. The many thousands of women who have not put themselves in this position see that there is the support to deal with the legal system without being rendered completely powerless in the process.

On New Year's Day 1983, 44 women were arrested and also charged with breach of the peace when they went over the fence at Greenham and climbed on to a missile silo still under construction. Thirty-six of these women refused to be bound over to keep the peace and were also sentenced to 14 days in prison in February. In this case it was decided to call women expert witnesses: Dr Rosalie Bertell from Canada who gave evidence about the far-reaching and long-term effects of low-level radiation; and Dr Alice Stewart, an epidemiologist, who has studied deaths from US atomic tests in the Pacific.

The action of closing the base on 13 December 1982 proved there are thousands of women willing to take this kind of direct action. As a result, the tactics of the police and courts have changed at least for the time being. Magistrates now seem to have decided to make any punishment as light as possible, if the charges cannot be dismissed entirely, in an attempt to damp down further publicity

Meeting women out of Holloway, March 1983

and support for the women. In some cases confused or contradictory police evidence has also made it impossible to uphold the charges. Women went on to the base at Greenham many times between New Year's Day and Easter 1983, though not on to the silos. Most of them were not charged at all. Sometimes they were taken to the police station and later released. On other occasions they were merely removed from the base. The group who lay down in Downing Street in February while the US Vice-President, George Bush, dined with Margaret Thatcher, received conditional discharges after having been charged with obstructing the highway.

There is an important element of discretion for the police and the courts concerning what people are charged with and what punishments they get. While there may be legal precedents as guidelines, this area of discretion makes it possible for the authorities to vary their responses to the women's actions according to what seems to be in their best overall interests – even if this sometimes means not charging women who flagrantly break the law. Although we are not suggesting that the police and courts simply act on government 'instructions', this suggests co-ordination between them.

It is interesting that the law and the established media, both neutralising the women's action in their different ways, sometimes work together and sometimes against each other. Journalists are invariably angry when they are not allowed into court. Their interest in some of the actions and their reporting of arrests and imprisonment has done a lot to fuel the whole campaign, which in turn has resulted in this apparently more lenient approach by the police and the courts, as they try to minimise opportunities for further publicity. At the same time the media also support the workings of the law – for example, by not reporting the women's most challenging court statements, or, in their reports of the first two evictions, by omitting to mention that the women stayed on.

Reliance on petty by-laws concerning property and land ownership is one way in which the authorities refuse to acknowledge the political nature of the women's peace camp. By contrast, the women have used the courts and legal proceedings to their advantage, refusing to be sucked in to what they think of as irrelevant discussions.

Something that rarely reaches the newspapers is the atmosphere of these court cases. We hear much about 'tears' and 'emotional scenes' but little about the manner in which women choose to conduct their defence. At the injunction and possession order hearings in March 1983, for example, hundreds of women gathered outside the court. The court room was full of defendants, so many they had difficulty fitting in. The women refused to be intimidated by legal niceties, thus making the rigid, authoritarian principles which guide court procedure simply ridiculous. Each woman has the opportunity of justifying her actions to the court and uses this to make a personal statement. These statements are an integral part of the proceedings. Woman after woman gets up to explain what her action means for her, recounting dreams, putting direct questions to the magistrates, telling personal histories and discussing personal priorities. These statements allow individual women to put their case on their own terms to the court and potentially the public.

When we lay down in the sewer pipe trenches, we took an action to make the men fully aware of what they are doing. The men found it difficult to look at us because they understood what we were trying to achieve. They don't want a nuclear war to happen, but because they have no alternative, we are forcing them to work at the base . . . We can be sent to prison, treated like criminals, because we do not want to see our families or any other individual on this planet obliterated by nuclear devastation.
Helen John, 17 November 1982

Time is running out. People have to realise and face the drastic situation . . . British people and people all over the world have been protesting legally for 40 years and it hasn't worked. Britain's economy is falling to pieces because of nuclear weapons. We still have more per square mile than any other European country. Cruise missiles are the limit – the last straw. They are illegal. They contravene international law.
Charlotte Kiss, 17 November 1982

In February, three women were arrested for blockading an entrance to the base at Greenham. They were charged with obstruction and faced a small fine. In order to make their statements public, however, and to take part in public discussions about nuclear weapons, they decided not to appear in court to be judged by the magistrates, but to hold a public meeting instead. They publicised their reasons in a letter to The *Guardian* (11 March 1983):

Sir – The *Guardian* reported (4 March) the trial of women at Newbury Magistrates' Court charged with wilful obstruction at Greenham Common.

We did not appear in court – we preferred to present our case to an open meeting that day at the Mound in Edinburgh – for the following reasons:

On 15 February, 44 women appeared at Newbury, charged with breach of the peace. They had been arrested for singing and dancing on the silos being built to house cruise missiles at Greenham Common.

They were found guilty, and 39 of the women have since served 14 days in Holloway for refusing to be bound over. At their trial the women presented a mass of evidence justifying their actions by proving that the introduction of cruise missiles is a criminal step towards genocide.

We believe that if their case had been decided by public opinion, their action would not have been condemned as a crime, but supported as a valid and urgent protest against the crimes being carried out in our names, but without our consent, at Greenham Common, military bases, and nuclear research centres throughout the world.

The courts, in trying and condemning people arrested for protesting against nuclear weapons, are trying and condemning the validity of direct action, that is, our right to be involved in the decisions which affect our lives when we are denied representation; and the validity of our arguments, that is, whether nuclear weapons are necessary or acceptable in our society.

We believe these issues are beyond the jurisdiction of the courts.

At the trial of the 44 women, three magistrates assumed the responsibility of public judgement, but passed verdicts unrepresentative of public opinion. Evidence presented to the court could not be reported to the public outside.

We were arrested, with the 14 other women who appeared in court, for blockading traffic entering the base at Greenham Common during action in support of the 44 women on trial. We were charged with 'wilfully obstructing the highway without lawful authority or excuse'.

In law, the desire to prevent the negligent destruction of our world as we know it is insufficient excuse for obstructing traffic. In law, we have no alternative but to plead guilty to the offence as charged. In law, our case is decided even before our trial and, unlike the 44 women, we would be given no opportunity to offer evidence in our defence, only in our mitigation, thus admitting our guilt.

We do not accept that we are guilty of any crime, nor do we accept that a magistrates' court is the appropriate place to judge our actions.

The Edinburgh meeting – having heard our statements and

evidence from others against nuclear weapons – found us not guilty of any crime.

Yours sincerely,

Shara Hanna, Louise Robertson, Jenny England,

Faslane Peace Camp, Argyll

These women were arrested again a few days after this, however, and taken to Newbury Magistrates' Court. They were given a small fine for the obstruction but sentenced to 14 days imprisonment for failing to appear in court when summonsed. The usual punishment for failing to appear is a £5 to £10 fine. This is a telling example of the importance of the court's discretion. By contrast, charges were quietly dropped against two of the 44 women involved in the silo action who did not turn up in court – the only difference being that they did not publicise the fact.

Despite the vast body of law at their disposal and their access to the media, the authorities have so far completely failed to intimidate the women or to silence them. It is difficult to speculate on how they will respond as the campaign continues to grow.

What are you doing to keep the peace? The power you are using is supporting nuclear weapons. It supports binding women's voices, binding our minds and bodies in prison so our voices cannot be heard. So our warning of Death is being repressed. But we cannot be silenced. And I cannot be bound over. I am asking you to keep the peace. We are not on trial. You are.

Katrina Howse, 17 November 1982, addressing Newbury magistrates.

Pam Isherwood

Ending

The symbol most closely connected with the women's peace movement is the weaving of webs. Each link in a web is fragile, but woven together creates a strong and coherent whole. A web with few links is weak and can be broken, but the more threads it is composed of, the greater its strength. It makes a very good analogy for the way in which women have rejuvenated the peace movement. By connections made through many diverse channels, a widespread network has grown up of women committed to working for peace. Greenham Common women's peace camp has been one thread in the formation of this network, showing the clear-sightedness and determination that so many women feel over the issue of nuclear weapons.

Women at the 1981 Women's Pentagon Action wove webs around the doors of the Pentagon, symbolically closing them, and this activity has since been used elsewhere. It has been taken up by women partly because it sets up such clear opposition. Police, for example, are trained to deal with force and aggression, not to extricate themselves from woollen webs. Thus, the confrontation that develops is very direct yet nonviolent and on women's terms. Images of gates shut with wool rather than iron bolts, and women being lifted out of webs are also graphic illustrations of polarised philosophies: those planning nuclear destruction, and those determined to preserve life.

To oppose nuclear weapons requires a fundamental change in our attitude to life. Clarity of purpose and utter opposition is the only chance to reverse the threat that hangs over all our lives.

What we want to change is immense. It's not just getting rid of nuclear weapons, it's getting rid of the whole structure that created the possibility of nuclear weapons in the first place. If we don't use imagination nothing will change. Without change we will destroy the planet. It's as simple as that.
Lesley Boulton, June 1982

The way things are organised is neither natural nor inevitable, but created by people. People have a wealth of skill, intelligence, creativity and wisdom. We could be devising ways of using and distributing the earth's vast resouces so that no one starves or lives in abject poverty, making socially useful things that people need – a society which is life-affirming in all its aspects.

For more information:

Books
Joel Kovel, *Against the State of Nuclear Terror*, Pan 1983.
Paul Rogers, Malcolm Dando and Peter Van Den Nungen, *As Lambs to the Slaughter: The Facts about Nuclear War*, Arrow 1981.
Gwyn Prins (ed.), *Defended to Death*, Penguin 1983.
Jonathan Schell, *The Fate of the Earth*, Picador 1982.
Nicholas Humphrey, *Four Minutes to Midnight: The Bronowski Memorial Lecture*, BBC Publications 1981.
The Greenham Factor, Greenham Print Prop 1983.
Susan Koen and Nina Swaim, *A Handbook for Women on the Nuclear Mentality*, Women's Action for Nuclear Disarmament 1980.
John Hersey, *Hiroshima*, Penguin 1946.
Lynne Jones (ed.), *Keeping the Peace*, The Women's Press 1983.
J. Humphrey, Dr M. Hartog, Dr H. Middleton, *The Medical Consequences of Nuclear Weapons*, Medical Campaign against Nuclear Weapons 1981.
Dr Helen Caldicott, *Nuclear Madness*, Bantam 1980.
Feminists against nuclear power, *Nuclear Resisters*, Publications Distribution Co-operative 1981.
Peace News, fortnightly magazine, 8 Elm Avenue, Nottingham 3.
Piecing It Together, Feminism and nonviolence study group 1983.
Pam McAllister (ed.), *Reweaving the Web of Life: Feminism and Nonviolence*, New Society Publishers 1982.
Raymond Briggs, *When the Wind Blows*, Hamish Hamilton 1982.

Films and videos
Critical Mass, 40 mins, videotape of talks by Dr Helen Caldicott; and *If you love this planet*, 25 mins, 16 mm film of Dr Helen Caldicott, both distributed by Concord Films Council, 201 Felixstowe Road, Ipswich, Suffolk IP3 6BJ. Concord Films Council has over 200 films about militarism, noviolence, nuclear weapons, the arms race, etc. available for hire.
America: from Hitler to MX, 90 mins, 16 mm film and video about the arms industries in the US. The Other Cinema, 79 Wardour Street, London W1.
Commonsense: Actions 1982, 40 mins, Super 8 film and video of women's nonviolent direct action, London Greenham office, see below.

Addresses
Women's Peace Alliance, Box 240, Peace News, 8 Elm Avenue, Nottingham 3.
Women's Peace Camp, USAF/RAF Greenham Common, Newbury, Berkshire.
Women for Life on Earth, 2 St Edmunds Cottages, Bove Town, Glastonbury, Somerset.
Women Oppose Nuclear Threat, Box 600, Peace News, 8 Elm Avenue, Nottingham 3.
London Greenham Office, 5 Leonard Street, London EC2.
Campaign for Nuclear Disarmament, 11 Goodwin Street, London N4.